Death Without Denial
Grief Without Apology

Life is a gift
Live fully.
Cherish your
special Memories.

Barbara Roberts

Death Without Denial
Grief Without Apology
❧

A GUIDE FOR FACING DEATH AND LOSS

Barbara K. Roberts

FOREWORD BY
Ann Jackson
Oregon Hospice

Compassion in Dying of Oregon

NEWSAGE PRESS
TROUTDALE, OREGON

NewSage Press
PO Box 607
Troutdale, OR 97060-0607
503-695-2211

website: www.newsagepress.com
email: info@newsagepress.com

Cover Design by George Foster
Book Design by Patricia Keelin

Printed in the United States on recycled paper with soy ink.

Distributed in the United States and Canada by
Publishers Group West 800-788-3123

Library of Congress Cataloging-in-Publication Data

Roberts, Barbara, 1936-
  Death without denial, grief without apology : a guide for facing
death and loss / Barbara K. Roberts ; foreword by Ann Jackson.
    p. cm.
  ISBN 0-939165-43-0
  1. Death--Psychological aspects. 2. Terminally ill--Psychology. 3.
Loss (Psychology) 4. Grief. I. Title.
  BF789.D4 R58 2002
  155.9'37--dc21
                            2001007552

1 2 3 4 5 6 7 8 9 10

In memory of my husband, Frank Roberts

CONTENTS

ACKNOWLEDGMENTS

Starting a book is certainly a daunting task and the emotional tone of this book adds to that challenge. So let me lovingly acknowledge my late husband Frank Roberts, my parents Bob and Carmen Hughey, my children's father Neal Sanders, and my sister Pat Welter. In four short years these five people I love so, caused me to see death, *face* death, *accept* death, and finally, in the case of my sister, watch death *cheated*. Without love and this painful set of losses, this book would never have happened.

I thank the Willamette Valley Hospice Program of Salem, Oregon and its walk-on-water staff. You taught me that death does not have to be about physical pain, about denial, or about isolation. I will be forever grateful for your gentle and patient lessons.

In the years I spent writing this book there were times when it seemed too painful to pursue it any further. My loving thanks to those who listened, read, and encouraged me to stay the course: Persis Whitehouse, Geoff Sugarman, Nancy Wakefield, Terry Bean, Ann Jackson, George Eighmey, and my special cheerleader, Rod Patterson.

In February 2001, Maureen Michelson, publisher of

NewSage Press and I sat down to tea in a quaint Japanese restaurant. I brought my manuscript and high hopes. Maureen brought a discerning eye for possibility, a wonderful heart for caring about the subject matter, and a honed talent for editing a first-time author. I desperately needed all of her skills. I thank her for her patience, clarity, understanding, and mentoring. And I especially thank her for being able to visualize the book cover my heart needed to complete this project.

My thanks and constant amazement over Jay Harter's magic with my computer. Your willingness to be there whenever I called for help was a lifesaver. And a special acknowledgment to the book designers at NewSage Press who so beautifully and professionally brought this book to reality: cover designer George Foster, and book designer Patricia Keelin.

My special thanks and gratitude to those who helped care for Frank during his last illness. Without Arlene I couldn't have done it. You are the kindest most gentle caregiver I have ever known. To Chuck, Celia, Roger, Mary Beth, Laurel, Donna, Nancy, Leslie, Rex, Cecelia, and the entire hospice staff: You brought warmth and love into a season of gray. I won't ever forget.

To Peter and Gratten who read to Frank, and to Terry who brought music to his bedside, my permanent gratitude.

To Rick and Laurel who served Frank with such

devotion in that final legislative session, my love and great appreciation.

And a special salute to the officers of the Oregon State Police who were there time after time for Frank and Arlene and me.

To my two sons, Mike and Mark and my grandchildren, Katie and Robert, please know the depth of joy and love you add to my life. You are my sunshine!

And finally, to Compassion in Dying of Oregon and George Eighmey and Barbara Coombs Lee, my deepest thanks for making my hawk real. You freed the hawk to fly.

— Barbara K. Roberts
Portland, Oregon

FOREWORD

It is not easy for Americans to talk about dying. We do not know what to say, afraid we will say the wrong thing or ask "stupid questions." We ignore warning signals, delay completing advanced directives, or writing wills. We do not want to hear "bad news." We wait. We deny.

However, polls reveal that we think about dying. If sick, we want to know if our life expectancy is limited. We want to die at home and receive the kind of care that hospice provides. We fear dying in pain, being hooked up to machines, or impoverishing our families.

Unquestionably, we all need advocates. *Death Without Denial, Grief Without Apology* teaches us how to be advocates for ourselves and for our loved ones when we face a life-threatening illness. Barbara Roberts provides accurate and timely information that will help us make good, end-of-life decisions for ourselves or for someone we love. If we do not seek information and ask questions, we can create a potentially devastating communication gap. Oftentimes, we wait for our doctors to tell us the bad news, but our doctors remain silent, waiting for us to ask the questions. To close that gap, we must give one another permission to be open and honest in our communications about diagnosis, treatment options, and life expectancy.

I learned this on a personal level when, after working with Oregon Hospice for nearly eight years, I faced the impending death of my fiancé, John, and I became his caregiver. Had I not known about hospice, end-of-life options, and pain and symptom management, the last stages of my fiancé's illness may have been very different. John needed an advocate, and I knew how to advocate on his behalf until he died on October 23, 1996.

Ten days later, I returned to my work as Executive Director of Oregon Hospice. While I knew a lot about dying, I knew little about grieving. I had not talked with anyone who had gone through what I was going through—the loss of a partner. Although I worked with an enlightened group—people who were comfortable talking about death—we did not talk about the death of my fiancé and my grieving. I waited for them to ask, but most did not even know! In addition, friends and acquaintances were uncomfortable if I talked about John, so I did not talk about him, and a great silence surrounded my mourning.

I needed an advocate to help me face my grieving, and I found that advocate three months later when I first spoke with Barbara Roberts. From the first time I told Barbara about John's death, my "healing" began. Barbara encouraged me to talk, and she listened. She felt what I was feeling. She talked about her own grieving process, and she gave me permission to be weird as I worked through my own grieving. I will always be grateful to Barbara.

Barbara Roberts's husband, Oregon State Senator Frank Roberts, died in hospice care on October 31, 1993, in the governor's residence. A few weeks before his death, Governor Barbara Roberts signed into law Oregon's Health Care Decisions Act. This Act remains one of the most progressive advanced directive laws in the country. In addition, as of January 2002, Oregon continues to be the only state in the nation to have a physician-assisted death law in place, first approved by voters in 1994, and operational since 1998. And as this book goes to press, the federal government is challenging Oregon's "Death with Dignity" law.

As a result of her personal journey through the death of loved ones and grieving, Barbara Roberts has responded to a growing need for open communication about death and dying. *Death Without Denial, Grief Without Apology* is her response. This is a touching story about love and loss, and grief and growth. Roberts's book tells the story that hospice people know needs to be told.

— Ann Jackson
Executive Director, Oregon Hospice
November 2001

INTRODUCTION

This is a book I *felt* long before I wrote it. I wanted to write in plain language so that others might find a source of comfort from my experiences and ideas learned during my husband's terminal illness and in my period of grief following his death.

I make no pretense that I bring any special expertise to the subject of death and grieving that is not also understood by professional grief counselors, psychologists, psychiatrists, mental health counselors and religious professionals. Because grief and healing and loss are such private journeys, we often seek something we can carry with us, keep beside our bed, turn to in moments of overwhelming emotional pain, refer to when no one else seems to understand our feelings and thoughts.

It is my hope that this volume may offer you a comforting way to think about what has happened (or is happening) to you. May this book cushion in some small way your battered emotions and help you to choose your own path, even your own temporary crutches on this difficult trip. I can only offer you words and thoughts on these pages. Please understand that, if I could, I would be that hand in yours, that gentle but lengthy embrace that you may need a hundred times a day.

At no time in your life will human warmth and contact feel more essential and yet at no time will you feel more isolated and removed from that which you need.

I hope for a culture of loving openness in every medical office, hospital room, health care clinic, and emergency room where news of life's limitations and death's impending arrival are discussed openly and compassionately. People who are dying and their families and loved ones must be prepared to create such a culture for themselves. The more openly and directly you face your diagnosis, the stronger chance you have of controlling your life choices.

May this book offer you something for your mind, your heart, your spirit, and your healing.

Death Without Denial
Grief Without Apology

ONE

A Culture in Denial

I stood in the doorway of the large bedroom staring toward the windows. But I did not see the winter trees beyond the glass, the now-empty bird feeders in the late sun, or even the dark oak that framed the windows and the window seat in the warm and inviting room.

I saw only a single white rose and a sprig of pine in a small vase on the window ledge next to a lovely piece of sculpture. Three shiny bronze dolphins played and leapt in the metallic waves of the art piece. For a long time I stood looking at the sculpture, imagining the dolphins' sounds and sensing their freedom. Then silently, once again, the tears began.

This was no ordinary room. It was the bedroom where my husband had died six weeks earlier. The sculpture was the urn I had chosen so carefully—a tribute to him and to the sea he loved. I had placed the urn containing Frank's ashes on the window ledge, near the outside bird feeders. When Frank could no longer go outdoors, he had watched the birds from his bed. The bed where he died was next to his big chair, near the large dresser with the framed family photographs he had requested.

His urn was on the window ledge,
but I couldn't tell anyone.

Frank died on Halloween and he would be interred on his birthday, December 28th. I brought him home for Thanksgiving and Christmas. Construction workers were finishing a new room at the mausoleum where his remains would be placed in a few more weeks. But especially during this season, I couldn't face the thought of Frank's urn in the dark and lonely mausoleum vault. Frank was home for the holidays. But I couldn't *tell* anyone.

So I stood crying in the lovely big bedroom, alone with his ashes, the devastating memories of his death—and my secret life of grieving.

And then I did what I did every afternoon. I walked over to his urn, put both hands on this lovely art piece and said, "Hi, Honey. I'm home." In this room, this sanctuary, I could still talk to Frank, report about my day, kiss his photograph, and wrap myself in his robe. Here, holding his urn in my lap, I could tell him how I struggled through each day without him.

So I ask myself if more than seven years after Frank's death in 1993, is this the story one dare tell to strangers—or even friends? Are these the actions of an emotionally stable person? Will people who know me, reading this book, shake their heads? The answer is, I can't worry about these questions if I am going to write about the grieving process with any honesty or validity.

I cannot hide from public view these uncomfortable stories and be of any real help to people who read this. For it is in the telling of such stories that I began to free myself from the cultural bondage of "appropriate" grieving and allowed myself the normal and natural experiences I needed to heal. I do not know who made these rules about "appropriateness." I only know they are wrong. When we share our grief stories, we help free not only ourselves, but we free our society from the silence and isolation that has long surrounded death and grieving in this country.

When my father died unexpectedly in 1990, a friend gave me a wonderful book about loss. *To Heal Again* by Rusty Berkus is primarily a picture book with bright, Japanese-like illustrations and minimal text. From my first reading of this book, two thoughts stayed with me, and sustained me:

> *Grief will take as long as it takes.*
> *There is no right way to grieve—*
> *there is just your way.*

When I read these words it was as if this book gave me permission to grieve in my own time and in my own way. Those words imprinted on me and they have become my belief.

Unfortunately, we live in a society that seldom gives us such permission. We are surrounded by a culture afraid to use the words *dead, death, died,* or *dying.* Instead we say loved ones "pass on" or "pass over." They are "deceased," "gone," "in heaven," or "on the other side." People are "no longer with us," "sleeping forever," and have "passed away." She "lost" her son in a car accident. Their daughter was "taken from them" due to cancer. An old bowling partner "kicked the bucket." Your Army buddy "bought it" in Vietnam. And the list goes on.

Dying and *dead* are words that seem so final, so harsh, in a society unused to hearing them. A patient is "terminal" rather than dying. A doctor is inclined to say, "He has six months," rather than "He will die before summer."

Yet, it is only when you can say the words or write the words or hear the words, that you can set aside denial and begin the healing process. Part of the healing process surrounding death is to come to terms with your loss, to accept that your loved one is gone. Acceptance begins by simply saying the death words. Yet our culture postpones that reality by word and by deed.

We send dying patients to hospitals to be hooked up to heart monitors, blood pressure systems, intravenous feeding devices, catheter tubes, and respirators. In most cases, none of these medical interventions matters or even makes sense. What a dying person needs is comfort, closeness, dignity, and in some cases, pain control.

Hospitals are isolating, intrusive, and expensive for the dying. They often hide the reality that death is approaching. Hospitals give us the sense that we are doing the right thing. We think of a hospital as a place one goes to get well. We often expect miracles there. Nurses, clean white sheets, sanitation, and flower deliveries imply recovery. Thermometers, patient charts, visitors' hours, and doctors reassure us that we are "doing everything possible."

Everything but what most dying patients would choose. *Home!* The sound and smell of the familiar, one's own bed, family, animal companions, cherished surroundings, and personal choices are tremendous comforts when dying.

Traditionally, doctors are trained to sustain life, not plan for death. However, if the doctor would say "dying" to a patient, the pretense of recovery would be gone. If a spouse or life partner says "dying" to a loved one they are then free to plan, share, and say goodbye over days or weeks or months. The dying person could then speak the truth to old friends, thank parents, prepare children. Conversations could be real. Expectations would be expressed. Fears could be shared. Memories could be made that would sustain and comfort those left to grieve once death arrives.

Our culture must stop whispering, hiding,
and turning away from death and grief.

And if death due to aging or disease is not bad enough in this respect, even worse is this society's reactions to a death caused by drugs, AIDS, suicide, or family violence. In these cases, when family members are desperate for words of comfort and understanding there is silence. These are the "if only" deaths. Loved ones have the extra burden of believing they could have prevented the death, "If only... If only...."

We must no longer be afraid to challenge a culture that expects silence on the subject of death, a culture that closets the process and then once death happens, asks us to grieve privately and quickly. We are expected to "move on," to "get over it."

Life is too precious and grieving is too important to permit the delegation of dying and mourning to a closeted experience. The art of living and the art of dying are equally significant. Grieving is an intimate part of both.

If you are questioning whether it is okay to grieve in your own way, then I give you permission to weep, weep loudly. Take his sweatshirt to bed. Talk about her and to her. Keep pictures in the living room and set an empty place at the table. Watch old movies and videotapes that show that *familiar* face. Hug a pillow and rock yourself. Put your feet in his shoes or wear her ring on a chain under your clothing next to your skin. Cry out his name in the night, visit her grave as often as you need to. Do the things that help you through a night, a day, a week, a year, two years. Through all of this remember, "It will take as long as it takes."

You are not crazy. You are mourning. These and other

personal grieving rituals can help you through this long and lonely process. You need not apologize for feeling, for hurting, for struggling, or for continuing to love and long for someone who has died.

You do not need my permission or anyone else's permission to grieve, but in a culture that frequently withholds that permission, I want to make clear that you are free to mourn your loss.

Do not let anyone tell you otherwise.

TWO

The Many Faces of Death

The faces of death are many: Quick or slow. Young or old. Violent or peaceful. Accidental or intentional.

In Chapter One, I referred to the "if only" deaths. These are deaths where we feel we might have prevented the tragedy in some way—a suicide, a child's drowning, a battered woman friend, a drug overdose, an alcohol-related accident. But, like all deaths, even those with this extra sense of guilt, we must move through the long, slow process of grief and healing. Almost every death leaves us with the hindsight that we could have done more, given more, said more. What I describe as "the work of grieving" includes coping with the intertwined burdens of guilt, loss, and loneliness. Braided together, they represent "grief work." For each one of us this work will vary.

If you ask people to comment on the best way to die the most frequent answers are: "In my sleep." "Quick." "While making love." Most people are equally clear that death without pain, death outside a nursing home, and death prior to major physical or mental deterioration is preferred.

Unfortunately, many of those choices may not exist for us or for those we love. Disease, accidents, and complications from aging are a part of life. And I now believe that it is healthy to accept the "how" of a loved one's death—which is ultimately beyond our control—and leave our energy and emotions free to focus on grieving and healing.

My father was a blue-collar guy with great warmth and tenderness. I adored him every day of my life. As long as I can remember he always said, "When I go, I want it to be fast." He watched five sisters die of cancer. He didn't want to experience that kind of a death. He got his wish.

I spent one particular Saturday working with Dad near

the end of a demanding election campaign in my race for governor. Time with my father always buoyed my spirits and renewed my energy. On that day we were at the Salem Senior Citizen Center where he was a Meals-On-Wheels volunteer. He glowed with pride from the front row when I spoke to the audience. He was especially pleased when I spoke about him. "Your senior citizen's center is a special place for you to be involved in so many enjoyable activities. But even more than that, it is seniors supporting seniors. The dozens of seniors who volunteer for Meals-On-Wheels is a perfect example. And my favorite Meals-On-Wheels volunteer is here today—my dad, Bob Hughey. He has been my role model for helping others in times of need. Without his caring examples, I might not be here today as a candidate for governor. Good parents are a remarkable asset and I've had one of the best."

When I left the center, I gave him a big hug. As I held him for a long time, I noticed how thin, even frail, Dad felt in my arms. Then I went off to another rally and he went out with a crew to put up political lawn signs for me.

Early the next morning my sister called. They were rushing Dad to the hospital in an ambulance. She didn't think he was going to survive. I was an hour away. Before I could reach the hospital, he died.

At the time, it felt as if I did not have a chance to say

goodbye or to tell him again how much I loved him. No chance to tell him what a wonderful father he was and how proud I was to be his daughter. Three weeks later, he wasn't there to share my victory when I became the Governor of Oregon. How Dad would have loved that celebration!

Forever I will regret that my father's death happened so quickly that my first goodbyes were in an emergency room cubicle when he could no longer hear me. His skin was already cold. But Dad got his wish to die quickly, and that's more than many of us will get.

While grieving the death of my husband, I learned that I could also continue to say goodbye to my father and tell him I loved him, and thank him—as many times as I needed to. And I have.

When my husband was dying, slowly deteriorating from the effects of his cancer, I often thought of my father. I thought how quickly death came for Dad and I longed for Frank to have a swift release from his difficult process. But then I thought of what Frank and I had experienced in our last precious year together. We had so many opportunities to say goodbye and to express our great love for each other. I recalled all we had shared in that last year and what we had learned together. For me, as the one left to mourn, I no longer found my father's quick parting quite as positive by comparison. In light of the many conversations Frank and I shared, I sense he would feel much the same.

But, when all is said and done, there is no easy way.

THREE

The Diagnosis
and the Choices

In October 1992 my husband and I sat in the doctor's office waiting for the results of Frank's latest medical tests. This was not a new experience for us. Frank felt good and he was confident about this routine, six-month checkup. Yet, each time we faced this waiting with the same trepidation, the same anxiety. Frank was a four-and-a-half-year survivor of prostate cancer. It had not been an easy road. Frank's radiation treatments for cancer had severely damaged his spinal nerve system and he lost the use of his legs.

For the past four years he had dealt with constant pain

and two "dying" legs. He could never leave his wheelchair. Being a paraplegic was a tragedy but surviving advanced cancer for more than four years was a gift. Frank rarely complained about the price he paid for his survival.

But on *this* particular day his gift was to be withdrawn. The cancer had returned and spread. The doctor told us quietly that Frank's new condition, lung cancer, was terminal. "I'm sorry to report that your cancer has spread to your lungs. There is no good news here, Frank. This is a terminal condition. You've got about a year at the most."

One year! One year to live! The room was silent. I took Frank's hand. He squeezed my hand in return. Frank shut his eyes. No one spoke again for what seemed like a very long time. And then the doctor did something I will never understand. He told Frank he would set up an appointment for the following week to begin chemotherapy! Frank and I looked at each other—confused. And then Frank asked the two questions *every* patient in his position *should* ask.

"Will this treatment extend my life?" The doctor answered, "Yes." And then, the second critical question, the one that so often goes unasked. "For how long?" With some hesitation, the doctor answered, "A month maybe. Even six weeks."

If you are familiar with most patients' physical reaction to chemotherapy, you will know it is not a pretty picture. I have watched as the body reacts to this intentional poisoning. Chemotherapy is a harsh treatment. To undergo such treatment to perhaps extend Frank's life by four to six weeks seemed highly questionable. To undergo chemo would diminish almost all remaining quality of life from an already terminal patient.

For Frank, chemotherapy was not about cure. This was not about hope. This was certainly not about quality or reality or kindness. This was, and still is, a routine medical response to a cancer diagnosis. In most cases I believe this routine response is often a medical misjudgment encouraged by a culture in denial and a medical profession equally in denial and unwilling to treat death as normal.

We are so afraid of death in this culture, so geared toward "medical miracles," we seem to have lost all sense of perspective. There is nothing wrong with a patient wanting a medical miracle. However, we have come to a place where families are demanding miracles when death is imminent and doctors often play the Wizard of Oz trying to orchestrate false hope and deny reality. There comes a time when the medical community must lay all the information and facts and options on the table for a dying person to weigh. Then doctors and family members should step aside and defer to the patient's personal judgment and wishes— including the decision to stop treatment and face death on his or her own terms.

Frank said "No" to the treatment. He opted to maintain the most quality of life—and the most control possible—for the time he had remaining. He never regretted that decision.

That night after Frank and I received the devastating news that his cancer was terminal, we sat quietly together trying to cope with our emotions. We talked, cried, held each other. We tried to make sense of our situation. What should we do? Should we just go on normally? Should we stop everything and focus on the months he had left?

Finally, we came to two conclusions: We weren't ready to share the bad news with others and we needed to get away and together think out loud about our next steps.

We flew to Hawaii, a favorite place where we had often shared sunshine and happiness. For a week we asked ourselves all the tough questions. Together, we weighed and balanced dozens of important personal matters. Frank made choices. I made lists. When the emotional discussions became too difficult, we took a walk in the sunshine or sat in the moonlight watching the ocean. We found ways to balance the hard work with the beauty of the setting and the joy of our remaining time together.

Frank decided he wanted to die at home. He didn't want any more hospitals. We had some basic understanding of hospice care and decided when we returned home we would find out more.

Frank decided we would not tell anyone else about the diagnosis for several months except for immediate family and very close friends. Frank was a prominent member of the Oregon Senate and, in his public position, he didn't want to be treated as if he were dying—even though he was. The legislative session would begin in January and customarily would end in July. Maybe with his motorized wheelchair no one would be aware of his deterioration over those months. *Maybe.*

We made to-do lists. Write a new will, check insurance policies and retirement accounts. Did his insurance cover hospice care? Frank wanted to review all our financial commitments and debts. There were personal papers he needed to sort. Frank wanted to spend time with old friends before he became too ill to do so.

The list grew longer: names, telephone numbers, insurance agents, hospice. We even tackled the very first conversation about a memorial service (no funeral for him!) and Frank's very clear choice for cremation. As we talked each day, denial drifted further away. We took time out for a car tour on Maui with unsuspecting, longtime friends who lived on the island. We enjoyed the sunshine and each other as if it were the first time we had visited Hawaii. Every hour was magnified to greater importance now that we saw our life together within the framework of

Frank's impending death.

We had begun the hard work of acceptance. We were determined not to waste any time. The joys of sunshine, music, friends, and each other were paramount while adjusting to this terrible news. Now more than ever, these joys mattered. Frank was clear—he was going to *live* until he died. Accepting that he was dying gave Frank more space for creating good times. And, for those he would leave behind, he created more good memories.

We had begun the journey. I would travel with him every step of the way—until it was no longer possible.

During the early part of this journey I began to understand that clarity, compassion, and caring represented a safety net in a very difficult balancing act between acceptance and denial. Speaking at an AIDS care center one afternoon, I referred to it as "the art of dying." The gay community has been practicing this art form for years in the wake of the AIDS tragedy. The community has built support networks of nondenial as they help friends and loved ones die. Those who are dying and their loved ones have learned how to make the end of life into celebrations of love and friendship, music and humor. Patients' lives are filled with simple joys and fun, nearness and acceptance. AIDS patients have given us a role model for dying with courage, dignity, and truth.

There really is an art to dying. I have seen a kinder, gentler, and more realistic model for the end of life. It is time to help patients and their loved ones accept the realities of disease and illness and aging. *Kindness* is helping dying patients accept the diagnosis and then give them support and services to live the rest of their lives with as much dignity, as many choices, and as little physical pain as possible.

If your prognosis is not hopeful, how fortunate it is to have a doctor who will be honest enough and kind enough to give you the news clearly and directly. The news will never be easy but once it is delivered you will be left with surprisingly more choices than you might have imagined.

Your choices include whether or not to consider more medical treatment. Surgery, medication, or experimental options are yours, based on your belief in medical science, in technology, or new drugs. If after getting all your questions answered, you decide to proceed with medical interventions, that is your choice.

Or you may choose to change your lifestyle with the belief or hope that diet, exercise, meditation, or prayer may prolong your life and promote healing. You might also choose no treatment and opt to quit work and travel or write a book or spend full time with those you love. You may decide to use the time you have left to place your affairs in order, say good-bye to those important in your life, and quietly contemplate the dying experience you are beginning.

Some people who know they are dying choose to keep the prognosis secret for as long as possible. Others opt to tell their story to help prepare those close to them. Some people who are dying need a great deal of support. Others are pillars of strength, offering support to those around them.

The choices for approaching death are numerous. But I do strongly advocate selecting your path proactively rather than letting it happen by default or by letting your doctor choose for you. If you are dying, this is the time to act and plan and choose. You have been handed the priceless package of "advance notice."

Many dying people have no need for treatment or hospitalization. Instead, they need the comfort of home and of the familiar. Unnecessary medical treatment is not kind. False hope is not kind. Medical practitioners need to treat dying patients with the dignity of honesty so that "patients" can become "people" again, to use their remaining time in the happiest and most productive ways possible.

Denial is not your friend. Truth offers you more freedom and broader options. Denial is also costly. It uses up financial resources your family may need when you're gone.

Denial uses up chances to share your feelings with your closest loved ones. Denial wastes the life ingredient you can least afford to squander—time. So if you receive a terminal diagnosis and are given precious time before you die (rather than being hit by a truck or felled by a heart attack), seize the opportunity to face closure on *your* terms.

Create photographs and videotapes. Travel. Write letters to be read after your death. Have intimate conversations and special dinners with friends. Personally deliver gifts rather than leaving them for a legal executor to do. You can give or ask forgiveness for an old injury. Make time for quiet moments in the arms of a loved one. Build memories with your children and share stories with your grandchildren. Sunrises, sunsets, quiet walks, laughter, more stories, and expressions of love are still possible.

Life offers us few guarantees except death. Having advance notice of this inevitable journey gives one the chance to "pack" for the trip. And one can pack a great deal into a few months, even when dying.

Do not deny yourself these blessings by denying you are going away.

FOUR

Planning Ahead for Death

Preparing and planning for death and its aftermath will leave more space for survivors to focus on precious life memories when death arrives. That is the time for remembering not for planning.

Whether a death is expected or comes as a total shock, there are crucial steps each of us can take in advance. One of the most essential preparations you can make is a currently updated will. I emphasize "currently updated" since many wills unintentionally omit younger children or recently added grandchildren, or speak to concerns for now-divorced spouses. A special gift that was planned or promised is often neglected in the provisions of a will.

Wills can be simple or complex, speak to the obvious or make gifts that may surprise your survivors. Wills and codicils may itemize financial gifts, sentimental gifts, personal property distribution, and may be accompanied by written last words or even audio or videotapes. But whatever you decide to include in your will, it provides your beneficiaries with clear and personal guidelines.

Don't wait to write your will! You can change it or add to it later. But an out-of-date will or *none at all* can cause costly and painful issues for your loved ones.

A more delicate piece of pre-planning concerns what happens to your remains. Both terminal patients and healthy individuals have trouble dealing with these decisions. Family members often shun any such discussions. But, sooner or later, someone will make the choices. Here again, clarity saves money, and avoids uncertainty and anguish at the time of death.

In most states in America, cemetery plots, crypts, cremation, caskets, urns, and services may be selected, planned, and paid for in advance. But obviously, one must get past the denial of death's inevitability in order to do such pre-planning.

When my father died unexpectedly, my family was stunned. As the oldest child I took responsibility for the arrangements and how grateful I was to have the benefit of Dad's advance planning. We all knew he wished to be cremated. He had already chosen and paid for his crypt and urn several years earlier. What a burden was removed from my shoulders during this initial time of grief. And how financially easy the last preparations were for my mother. I will always be grateful to my dad for being such a considerate realist.

Now, as a result of that experience, I have purchased crypts for myself and both of my sons in the mausoleum where my parents' and husband's ashes rest. Most members of my family have been clear about their choices regarding cremation, burial, and services. Some people might think these pre-planning and pre-purchasing discussions are macabre. I like to think these decisions are realistic and based on kindness.

Another element of pre-planning is to be certain that your insurance policies, retirement accounts, and other related financial holdings have *current* beneficiaries on file. It is not unusual after someone dies to learn that the beneficiary was never changed from an ex-husband or that the youngest child was not added to the intended inheritance split of a deferred compensation account or an IRA.

Another small but helpful piece of pre-planning is to prepare an obituary or at least a biographical sketch so that others may use it for the newspaper announcement. Often children are surprisingly unclear about a parent's place of birth, military service, education, work experience, and even surviving siblings. A second spouse may lack that detail as well. The easiest way to assure accuracy on this final statement of your life is to have *you* provide the information.

Finally, on the subject of pre-planning, let me add this caution. If no one can put their hands on your insurance policies or your obituary or your will, all this kind, advance work may go to waste.

Your insurance policies, your will and obituary, your marriage license, birth certificate, military discharge papers, divorce papers, bank accounts, Social Security records, your documents for funeral pre-planning—all these papers should be in one, easy-to-access, safe place. At least two people should know where all the documents are located. Your survivors will need some of these papers right away and may not have the energy or emotional stamina to become a search party. Leaving all your documents and papers in order and readily available can be a final act of love.

The survivors, often deep in grief, may find themselves asking, "What am I supposed to do next?" Survivors must deal with mortuaries and death certificates, memorial services, sympathy cards and letters, insurance claims, Social Security forms, and so much more. And it all comes at the loved ones when they are *least* prepared to handle such details.

If you find yourself in this situation, here are a few suggestions. Do what *must* be done immediately and then get support or help for the items that remain. A friend can call and order the certified death certificates you will need for insurance companies, real estate titles, and Social Security. A friend or your attorney can help by notifying an insurance company or retirement account holder. You may find that you are not ready to write personal thank you letters. You may wish to have a thank you card printed that can be addressed and mailed to those who sent flowers, letters, food, or who helped in other ways. Friends or family members might share the chore of addressing these printed cards.

Remember that we often have friends and family who want to help, who want to ease the burden. Don't be uncomfortable in asking for their assistance and support. It will make all of you feel better.

Some people will bring food. Others will be able to help by answering the door or the telephone for you. If someone offers to do the laundry, that's okay, too. Take help from those who extend the offers. Take comfort from those who care about you. Too soon you will be left alone to cope with your loss.

But let me add this. In accepting help and support, do not let others push you into decisions you are not yet ready to make or do not wish to do at all. Well-intentioned friends and family may want to dispose of clothing or personal effects that you wish to have near you for awhile.

Sometimes people will want you to sell a home or move to another city or to sell a car right away. These are big decisions and unless finances make such immediate choices absolutely necessary, hold off on these major changes until you are better prepared to take steps that feel right for you long term. In your vulnerability after a major loss you may find it hard to resist pressure from a family member or close friend. But remember, this is your life and your adjustment as a survivor may depend on these very choices.

So if you are not ready to make such changes—say so! Most decisions can be delayed for at least a few months. Some decisions need not be made at all. The more survivors (especially widows and widowers) understand their own financial and personal situation, the better they can determine any major life changes and can delay uncomfortable choices until they feel prepared to handle them.

The bottom line is pre-planning is important, responsible, helpful, and realistic. It can take the worries off the shoulders of a dying person. Knowing that you have put your affairs in order can remove tremendous stress. Making financial arrangements and decisions about a final resting place can be comforting to a person facing death.

Pre-planning clarifies an individual's choices concerning memorial services, burial, cremation, obituaries, and religious options. Choices unspoken or unwritten are easily ignored.

Additionally, studies done in the United States have shown that funeral arrangements made in advance are less costly. In times of fresh grief, survivors make more expensive choices.

Every advance decision moves one further away from the possibility of denial, closer to the reality of impending death. For me, as difficult as the reality was, I breathed easier knowing the pre-planning was behind us. Frank felt very satisfied knowing that everything was in order. Pre-planning freed Frank's remaining time so we could concentrate on life and living.

FIVE

Hospice

My experience with the hospice program feels like a large beautiful quilt.

Each piece is a different color, shape, and fabric. Some memories I touch gently, feeling the sheen and softness of that particular experience. Other memories are rough yet add beauty and unique pattern. Some of these I can only glance at briefly before quickly looking away to more soothing, comforting parts.

My hospice quilt began in 1992 on an escalator in a shopping mall during the holiday season. As I viewed the scene from the slow-moving stairs, I focused on a fir Christmas tree covered with dozens of identical shiny metal ornaments. Two pleasant looking women sat near the large tree at a table with brochures, and a modest identifying sign that read "Mid-Willamette Valley Hospice."

As I arrived at the bottom of the escalator I was suddenly facing the tree and I realized that each shiny ornament was engraved with a name. I glanced away, moving quickly to avoid eye contact with the two women at the table.

Go buy another Christmas gift! Get in the spirit! I told myself. This would be a very important Christmas with Frank. I wanted everything to be perfect. Perfect. But how would I make someone's last Christmas perfect? Frank did not seem sick, even though his prognosis was terminal. By next Christmas he wouldn't be here. *Next Christmas Frank would be dead.*

I stopped, turned around, and walked back toward that special tree and the hospice table. A multitude of silver ornaments shimmered with reflected light—individual remembrances for loved ones, especially during this difficult season. I wrote a check so that my late father's name and ornament could be on the tree. *This hospice contact is about Dad and not about Frank,* I reassured myself.

I exchanged holiday greetings with the women at the table, picked up one of their brochures without looking at it, put it in my coat pocket and walked away. One more second and I would have been sobbing openly right there in the middle of the mall. I held my hand on the folded brochure in my pocket where the printed words soothed me as if they had been written in Braille.

The hospice brochure remained in my coat pocket for several days, unread. By New Year's Day it was in my bedside table, still folded, still unread. Each night as I climbed into bed, the brochure beckoned to me, waiting to be read. It reminded me of one of those movie cartoons where the item of temptation takes on a bright, pulsating glow that can be seen through the refrigerator door or through the closet door. But I simply couldn't muster the courage to read the small booklet.

I needed to understand hospice so Frank and I could talk about it and Frank could decide if it was right for him. But I also understood that this hospice choice was about me. What if Frank said "Yes" and then I didn't have the strength to follow through? What if I couldn't bear to watch him in pain, watch him deteriorate, watch him die at home? I had so many questions and I knew some of them would be answered in the brochure. I needed to read it soon. Soon!

When I finally opened the bedside drawer and took out the brochure, I noticed the logo for the first time. It was a circle with four layered sets of hills and then mountains and the words "Sharing the Journey." The first page began, "It's called Hospice." And then it explained in one sentence all I needed to know:

Hospice is a philosophy
of neither shortening nor prolonging life
but rather letting the terminal illness
take its natural course with care
and comfort of symptoms to provide the goal
of a peaceful death with dignity.

I read the sentence again. And then again. And then I devoured every word written in the brochure. My chest grew tight with emotional pain and unshed tears. I loved what the brochure said yet I hated what it meant for Frank and me. How could anything so painful be right for Frank? How could choosing something that seemed so right cause such wracking sobs? How could I discuss this pain and this confusion with strangers? I thought about it for a long time that night and then mentally added another piece to my hospice quilt.

Finally, I decided I would visit the hospice office—alone. I wanted to prepare myself for the discussion Frank and I would share later, and for the meeting that would likely follow between Frank and the hospice providers. Thank goodness for my decision to go alone! Three questions into my intended "professional" interview with the hospice director, I fell apart. Everything I was feeling came pouring out. Fear. Anger. Self-doubt. Frustration. Hopelessness. And a hundred questions.

The hospice director handed me a box of tissue, held my hand, held me. Clearly she had been here before with family members. When it was over I was totally drained but I felt ready to help Frank through this same set of questions, this same need to understand, this same valley. After that visit, I began to understand part of what the hospice logo meant about "sharing the journey."

Frank and I soon learned about the services available: medication, pain control, oxygen, patient bathing, respite care, volunteer help, equipment, counseling. As Frank grew more ill and his needs greater, hospice would be there to fill those growing needs: a hospital bed, liquid morphine, special bed pads, and bathroom equipment. Hospice emphasized that each new service or equipment would come with an explanation and supportive reassurance. Step-by-step we would learn.

We also found that hospice care was for all ages and any terminal diagnosis when life expectancy is initially predicted to be six months or less. Cancer, AIDS, Lou Gehrig's disease, kidney failure—whatever the situation, hospice was prepared to help. Financial coverage could be by insurance, Medicare, Medicaid, or on a sliding scale based on one's ability to pay.

But most importantly for me, the hospice staff made clear their commitment to help keep Frank free of pain. Hospice care is committed to the belief that the *quality* of life is as important as the *length* of life. Hospice staff works hard to give the dying person as many choices as possible, to help him or her feel in control until the end. When you are caring for a terminally ill patient it is easy to make decisions for him or her about what *you* think is best. It takes constant reminders to give your loved one every freedom possible. As a dying person begins to lose so much, this is something you can help him or her hold onto. Hospice continued to gently remind us of the need for personal choice throughout Frank's final months.

Within a few weeks of hospice's first visit to our home in February 1993, we made the decision. After many questions, reading, and talking, Frank knew this was the right choice for him. I couldn't have been more in agreement. I was scared and sad and had much to learn but I felt good about our decision. In the months ahead those good feelings would turn into a lifelong gratitude to hospice.

When we first began our actual working association with hospice in April, Frank was still going to the Oregon

State Capitol every day in his role as a state senator. Two or three times a week, the hospice nurse came at night to help Frank. Frank's motorized wheelchair allowed him to *appear* somewhat vigorous and active at work but each day he grew weaker. His increased weakness, pain, and breathing problems were not yet obvious to everyone. Our decision to keep his pending death a secret was still firm.

Once Frank arrived home each afternoon his world changed. Rest and sleep and pain medication were the late afternoon's first requirements. His food intake slowed down. He had trouble with his vision and reading. Frank's hands became weaker and shaky. Many nights neither he nor I slept longer than four hours. Hospice helped us understand all these changes and gave us the information and support to face what was happening. We always had new questions and they always offered useful explanations.

As Frank struggled with his increasing physical deterioration and his determination to complete his final legislative session, my own personal pressures and heavy job demands added to the weight of those months. I was in the middle of my first four-year term as Governor of Oregon.

My days were filled with back-to-back meetings and conferences, constant decision-making, traveling throughout the 97,000 square miles of Oregon, recognizing the varied issues of over three million Oregon citizens, and reading at least a briefcase full of reports and briefings every night. I also faced a grueling legislative session in full swing with way too little sleep and far too many personal worries.

As Frank's health issues grew worse, I traveled less, made fewer evening speeches, and found more ways to do part of my work at home. My personal and professional responsibilities seemed constantly on a collision course.

Several times every week I telephoned my two sons and Frank's two daughters to keep them posted on Frank's condition. Most of our five grandchildren were still quite young and had trouble understanding that their grandfather's illness was serious. The three grandchildren, all under age five, could hardly be expected to grasp the fact that their grandpa would soon be gone from their lives.

During this time of increased demands for help and support, Frank and I both felt fortunate to have a dear and long-term friend sharing our home. Only two years earlier Arlene had cared for her husband through his long illness and his death. Now, she was helping us through the same difficult process. Our respect and love for Arlene grew by the day and our gratitude immeasurable for this ultimate gift from a friend. To this day, Arlene and I remain the best of friends.

In June 1993, after months of silence, Frank publicly announced his latest cancer diagnosis and his plans to resign his state senate seat at the end of the legislative session. He could no longer be silent about what was happening to him. The physical and emotional costs of Frank's illness had become so taxing that honesty and directness came as a huge relief.

Soon everyone seemed aware of Frank's situation and we both talked openly and publicly about his terminal status, his choice to forgo further treatment, and his decision to make hospice his *final* medical caregiver.

In August, only two days after adjournment of the longest legislative session in Oregon history, Frank began to have serious trouble breathing. I rushed home from a meeting forty-five miles away. Hospice came immediately with oxygen equipment. But it turned out that the hospice counselor who came that day was almost as much of a lifeline as the oxygen.

Frank had never been in denial about his illness, but the oxygen requirement was a clear wake-up call that his time was narrowing. He was very upset and disturbed about it. Our bravery went temporarily out the window. Frank needed the oxygen but Arlene and I, too, felt near to hyper-ventilating. The hospice counselor talked with us for almost an hour. She asked about our fears and concerns. We all talked and held hands and cried, admitting how scared and shaken we all felt. Frank asked questions about what to expect next, and what further deterioration would be like. He wondered about being able to leave the house for his retirement dinner only days away. Arlene and I worried about operating the oxygen machine. What if the electricity went off? We were frightened that his need for an oxygen tank meant he could die at any time.

After we talked, Frank's courage and emotional strength returned. But his failing body was ready for rest. While Frank slept peacefully, the hospice staff again demonstrated their full support for family members, which is such an integral part of their caregiving. They assured Arlene and me, as his primary caregivers, that we had come through the crisis like troopers. We had faced reality, didn't panic, comforted each other, called hospice when we needed help, and we did not even hint at moving Frank into an alternative setting. Although upset for Frank, we remained committed to keeping him at home until the end. Frank felt safe and supported, and so did we. All my doubts vanished at that point. Hospice would be there for us. We would be all right, and we had clearly made the right choice.

Our reality changed that day. It was like looking through a pair of binoculars at our situation. Now death looked way too large and near, and time appeared small and out-of-focus.

During the next few weeks Frank's condition worsened. Even with oxygen his breathing was more labored. Frank's strength drained away and he needed help turning in bed. His retirement dinner would become his last time out of the house. He understood it was a farewell dinner. No one in the audience that night doubted that was the case. The physical price Frank paid for stretching his endurance to attend was overshadowed by the joy that evening brought him. Several hundred people came to celebrate his career, his contributions, and his life. The president of Portland State University announced an on-going graduate student scholarship in his name. Family, old friends, former students, fellow senators, and community leaders praised Frank, thanked him, and expressed their love and respect for him. Frank struggled through the evening both emotionally and physically. But whatever the physical cost may have been for Frank, he glowed in the love of this retirement dinner.

After that special night Frank slept more, ate less, and physically weakened. With his apparent decline and my increasing anxiety, I read and reread the hospice materials on pending death and the physical signs of a body shutting down. Some things I read were not quite clear until I saw them occur, especially when the hospice staff came daily to bathe Frank. The color began to leave his legs, moving from toe to knee to hip. His hands were less warm to the touch. We started to keep someone in Frank's room all night, trying to meet his every need. When he awoke in the middle of the night, I didn't want him to find himself alone. Until the end, we were committed to being at his bedside. But when that time might arrive, was an overshadowing uncertainty.

We shared bedside duty: Primarily Arlene and I, with help from close friends like Nancy, Chuck, Celia, Roger, Mary Beth, Laurel, Donna, and Leslie. And on the worst nights, our hospice nurse, Cecelia, arrived. Hospice staff and I worked with these friends, explaining how to keep Frank's pain under control, talk to him, reassure him, and in the event of a medical crisis to call hospice, *not* 911. Frank did not need a hospital or life support, and he definitely did not want resuscitation. He wanted relief from this long ordeal. His wishes were clear, his path was inevitable.

Three weeks before his death, Frank suffered a stroke. Hospice came immediately. They confirmed he had a stroke and that his speech was severely affected. Hospice described Frank's attempts to speak as "tossed salad." Frank was confused and frustrated. Hospice arranged for a speech therapist to come the next day to work with Frank.

Even though Frank's body and vision had been failing, and he was incapable of using his wheelchair any longer, his ability to speak had remained his outlet, his salvation—and our joy. Frank was a storyteller, a former speech professor with a wonderful imagination and an exciting vocabulary. Even on his worst days, his sense of humor was intact. Now, Frank was unable to communicate. For me, the day of Frank's stroke was one of the hardest days I faced. I had depended on his words to give me strength until the end.

Now, he could no longer speak.

That day I left Frank's bedroom and cried. *It wasn't fair. It just wasn't fair! Didn't he have enough to cope with already?* The hospice nurse comforted me, held me, and let me vent my pain. Then, quietly and kindly, Cecelia explained about some of the side effects of a body shutting down. "This stroke," she said, "is one of those effects, just like his colorless legs and his lack of food intake." A body shutting down didn't need new fuel. A body without fuel begins to close down. The time was narrowing.

For the next three mornings I made sure I was at Frank's bedside when he awakened. His inability to communicate made it difficult to know what he understood. So each morning I explained to him, "Frank, you've had a stroke and your speech is not clear. We'll do our best to understand you. Do you know what I'm saying?" For thirty-seven years Frank had taught speech communication as a college professor. So each morning I reminded him of that life experience in the hope he could call on that background to understand what had happened to him. "Frank, remember when you studied speech therapy at Madison and helped stroke victims learn to speak again? Can you help yourself speak again? Do you think you can do that?"

On the fourth morning after Frank's stroke, I was sitting on his bed when he opened his eyes. I went through my morning routine, explaining about the stroke and reassuring him that we would work hard to understand and help him. Then I asked him if he understood about the stroke. He paused a few seconds, gave me that endearing, mischievous smile of his, and reached his hand up to my face. Gently running his fingers across my cheek, he said clearly, "Stroke, stroke."

When I shared that story with the hospice staff over the next few days, we marveled together about Frank's resilience and humor. His speech improved and soon those shared stories became the buoys that I clung to in a sea of approaching loss. These stories would become some of my most special memories of Frank's last days and memories of the remarkable bond between our hospice team and our family.

As the days dwindled to a precious few, Frank needed more pain medication, more sleep, little food, almost total physical help, and lots of love. Our caregiving circle read to Frank, sang to him, talked to him, massaged his back, and added more and more pillows to his bed. Hospice came more frequently, held more hands, answered new questions, and readied us for what was coming. Hospice was clear that the end was approaching and helped us to prepare for the reality of our impending loss.

There was no denial about approaching death in the house. Some moments I would wish for all this to end for Frank. Other times I would sit beside him, watch him breathe, grateful for each breath. Sometimes in the night, restlessly dozing in Frank's big chair near his bed, I would suddenly get up, draw close to his bedside, and listen to him breathe. Reassured, I would gently touch his face. *Stroke. Stroke.*

Three weeks after Frank's stroke, all the signs of impending death that hospice had described were now evident. Family members began to gather. But there were no doctors, no injections or tubes, no intrusion—just Frank, his loved ones, and the hospice staff who I now thought of as the "wind beneath our wings."

The doubts I once had about having the strength, endurance, and emotional stamina to travel this road with Frank were gone. Hospice had given me the knowledge and wisdom to make this precious final journey with Frank in the most gentle, natural, realistic way possible. Forever, I will be grateful for Frank's decision and hospice's commitment to teach me about the art of dying.

To the end, hospice was always there for us. After Frank took his final breath, I looked at our hospice nurse who had stood at the foot of Frank's bed for hours. Our eyes held for a few seconds. Cecelia nodded "yes" to me, smiled gently, and then, as I had requested earlier, walked across the room and shut off the oxygen machine that had run constantly for two-and-a-half months. I have never known such silence.

Weeks later, an unusual thought occurred to me. In every personal situation I have experienced regarding someone's death—my grandfather, my niece, my father—and in every movie and television depiction of a death announcement, the people who delivered the news would always shake their heads back and forth sadly, meaning the person had died. Our hospice nurse had nodded "yes." "Yes, he is gone. Yes, this path we have taken together has led us to the destination we have worked toward for months. Yes, Frank's suffering has ended." I will never forget her affirmative nod, her gentle smile, and her final favor so I could hear the silence.

Hospice taught me not to dread the silence.

SIX

Caring and Caregiving

C aring for a dying person in the home is a difficult job, and a remarkable process. You are tested physically, psychologically, and emotionally, yet those who participate in this process are permanently and positively touched.

Many people are convinced they do not have the courage and personal strength required to do such caregiving. They look with awe at those who have chosen the caregiving path and believe that they possess special attributes not given to the rest of society. As someone who has walked this path let me assure you, more than courage and strength, the major ingredients for such caregivng are love and patience. You do not need to be a nurse, a saint or a hero—just a human being who cares and is willing to ask for help.

Let me be honest with you. The caregiving responsibilities for a loved one who is dying can test the patience of the most saintly among us. Do not begin this act of love without understanding that reality. And do not look back after the death, no matter what the process, and feel as if you have failed. Caregiving for a dying person at home is both a test of endurance and a demonstration of love. No one who assumes this responsibility will come out of it with a perfect record. Life and death are not about perfection.

You will change beds, lose sleep, and prepare food that is never eaten. You will lift the patient when your back aches and give nighttime pain medication when your emotional pain seems as terrible as your loved one's physical pain. Often you will sleep in a chair and eat when you have no appetite. And you will learn intimate details about bodily functions.

At the same time you will be privileged to hear the innermost thoughts of a person facing death. You will talk of love in the middle of the night. You will be there to give and receive comfort from a person who understands the priceless value of time. You will make space for sharing memories and slowly saying goodbye. And if you are lucky, you will be there to see your loved one slip comfortably and serenely into death.

Sometimes in the middle of the night I went to Frank's bed and often found him wide awake. I would ask if he needed something and he sometimes replied with answers such as, "No, I'm just thinking about my life," or "I was listening to the night," or "I need more time to be certain *you're* ready for this." I never knew what to expect from him in those quiet night visits. Those were the times when we would share some of our deepest thoughts.

One night Frank told me his concern about my impending loneliness. He thought that I should begin dating immediately after his death. Such a conversation allowed me to assure him I would be fine alone. During those private times we relived our many sailing adventures and talked of roads we had traveled together. We spoke of lovemaking and old friends and grandchildren—so many joys we'd shared in our twenty years. We touched, held hands, laughed, and asked questions not asked before.

Sometimes in the warmth of August and September Frank asked me to open his windows in the pre-dawn hours. He wanted to listen to the first morning songs of the birds at the feeders and the slight rustle of the trees just outside his bedroom windows. How he loved the birds! Until the end Frank drew tremendous joy and comfort from the birds' songs.

More than seven years later I still cherish the memories of those last weeks. How much I would have missed if Frank had been hospitalized and left in the care of professionals! I might have gone home at the end of visiting hours and missed learning about the night sounds.

With the high points of emotional sharing will come the counterbalance of some of the most stressful, trying times of your life. There will be times when you are tired, out-of-patience, and simply weary of the ordeal. You may say or do something that is less than kind, less than patient or understanding, less than caring. And when that moment has passed, you will feel ashamed. You will regret your act of frustration or weariness and the pain it may have caused your loved one. And, like a continuously playing film loop, the scene will replay in your mind. This is when you will have to learn compassion for yourself—and forgiveness.

But you cannot turn back the clock. You cannot retract your words or actions. And even if you apologized, you may be left with terrible guilt. I am still working on forgiving myself and replacing that guilt with the many positive memories of when I was truly there for Frank. There were difficult nights when I brought ice chips and rubbed them on Frank's parched lips, soothed his face with a cool wet cloth, and rubbed lotion on his back. Sometimes I sang to him and we cried together. Those are the memories that soothe and comfort me.

Not everyone can care for a patient at home and not

everyone will feel comfortable dying at home. Job responsibilities, family health issues, small children, special problems, or just plain fear may prevent home care. But if you and your loved one decide dying at home is preferable, I am confident you will be grateful for your decision.

For the rest of my life I will cherish my memories of caregiving, even though they were partly painful. I know Frank forgave my shortcomings and embraced my caring and love, and even my emotional strength as we daily faced his approaching death.

During the last weeks of his life, Frank had been clear with me that he was ready to die. Now it was my turn to be brave and to give him the permission he seemed to need. As Frank lay dying, surrounded by family, I had to help him let go. Our shared experience in the final weeks gave me the courage to do so.

With several deep breaths, I turned my thoughts to the majestic brown hawks of Oregon. I imagined the hawk in flight, soaring above the fields and hills, dipping and turning, beauty and freedom silhouetted against the sky.

Frank loved the brown hawk. He never failed to notice

one in flight. And a hawk perched like royalty atop a country split-rail fence post, never escaped his watchful gaze. The hawk was pure pleasure for Frank.

For our fifteenth wedding anniversary, I commissioned an artist to carve a life-like brown hawk for Frank. The small, carved wooden hawk sat on a fence post, rusted barbed wire curled around the post. Frank's special hawk nested on his office desk for five years until his death.

Kneeling on his bed that last early morning, I summoned all my courage and love and said softly, "It's time to let go, Frank. You can fly like the hawk, float on the air. The whole sky is yours. Be a hawk, Frank. You are free to fly now, my love."

I knew Frank heard me and understood. No longer did he need my caregiving. Now he needed me to demonstrate what I had learned in the last months about caring, loving, the night, the birds, and letting go.

And he let go and soared.

SEVEN

Facing Death:
The Misery and the Moment

There are some experiences where comprehension does not evolve from reading or hearing about them. Being there is the only way to understand. I have never read a description of a sunset that begins to do justice to the splendor and magnificence of its color and expanse. Standing in the night looking skyward during a snowfall creates a wonder of space and motion that one must experience to truly know. Witnessing the birth and first cry of a baby always causes me to weep, but I am without words to describe why.

For me, witnessing death is the combined experience
of sunsets, falling snow, and birth,
entwined into a soul-altering instant.

Like birth, I do not have adequate words to describe those last moments of life or the moment when breathing ends. Perhaps those are life experiences that insist on a knowing from the heart rather than the mind. Yet it is essential to give you some sense of that precious experience.

For several days it was clear that the end of Frank's life was near. He had not eaten for days, took little water, and was in a coma-like state. There was almost no bodily elimination and he seldom moved. Frank seemed unaware of the people who watched him closely and we tended to speak in whispers.

He was surrounded by pillows to keep him comfortable and physically supported. Frank looked small and pale in his nest of pillows. An oxygen tube helped him to breathe with more comfort and his pain medication was by his bedside, but even that seemed called for less and less. Our hospice nurse, Cecelia, was now in constant attendance and she felt Frank would not survive the next dawn.

The morning hours turned to afternoon and afternoon shadows gave way to darkness. Cecelia, Frank's two daughters, my younger son, and four other family members held vigil by Frank's bed. We waited and watched. We took turns holding

Frank's hand. Each glance across his big bed spoke volumes about trepidation, weariness, fear, and uncertainty. Quietly, we took turns comforting each other. As one person's courage waned another one of us found new strength for the difficult vigil. The swish and soft click of the oxygen machine was often the only noticeable sound in the room.

As the evening passed, it felt impossible for me to leave Frank's side. For long periods I knelt on Frank's bed so I could touch him, speak to him, comfort him. Hearing is the last sense to go for a dying person. I depended on that fact even when my words were unacknowledged. An hour passed, two hours, almost three. My legs were cramped, my back ached, but I was afraid to move. Finally, I had to leave Frank's side to use the bathroom. A wave of panic caught me.

How could I leave his side now? What if he died while I was out of the room? I didn't know what to do. We had begun this long trip together and now only a few steps away from completion, I couldn't be gone at the moment he died. Tears welled in my eyes. What could I do? Then I remembered what hospice had said about a dying person's ability to hear. So I simply told him, "Frank, I have to go to the bathroom. I can't wait. I will only be gone for a minute or two. You cannot die while I am out of the room. I want to be with you." I said it once, twice, three times. Frightened, I jumped off the bed, ran to the bathroom, and returned almost immediately to his bedside.

Then they told me. After four days without a word, Frank had spoken my name twice in that brief time I was out of his room. He had heard me. Frank knew I was there and he had waited.

A short time later, Frank began the final phase of his life. Hospice describes this as "apnea" which means alterations in the breathing pattern caused largely by decreased circulation. Breathing may not occur for ten to thirty seconds at a time. I had read the words "apnea" several times in the hospice materials but the description was meaningless until I witnessed it myself. And I will never forget the experience. Never.

The first time Frank stopped breathing we looked at the hospice nurse. She was looking at her watch then back to Frank. It was ten to fifteen seconds but it felt like an hour. Then Frank took another breath. Everyone in the room seemed to react—there were sighs, a small smile, a hand removed from a mouth. And then it happened again. This time the lapse between breaths was nearer twenty to twenty-five seconds. My stomach turned with fear. The pattern continued. Was it half an hour, an hour? I don't know and I have never asked. It seemed like days. Each time his breathing stopped I wondered if it would begin again. This was a body ready to die but a human being demonstrating the remarkable value of life, one breath at a time. Each new breath he took felt like a miracle.

Frank took another breath. We waited for the now-familiar pattern. Ten, twenty, thirty seconds. We waited for him to breathe again. My eyes left Frank's face to glance at the hospice nurse. She looked at her watch, then our eyes met. She smiled gently, nodded to me and then walked across the room to shut off the oxygen machine. The silence was deafening. Frank would not breathe again. I reached down and removed his oxygen tube. Then the silence was filled with sobs as we all understood the meaning of the quiet.

Later I realized that you cannot recognize someone's last breath when it happens. You only know it was a last breath when another does not follow.

I would not trade this painful, remarkable human experience for anything. I am so grateful for what Frank gave me, for what hospice helped me to understand and endure, and for the learning and growth I received from each person who was part of our journey.

After months of knowing and accepting and preparing and dreading, the end had come. The last breath, the silence, the shock of death's reality. Numbness came almost immediately. I cried, comforting others in the room, allowing them to comfort me. But as I wept I felt as if I was viewing this scene from outside myself. I watched as the hospice nurse quietly went about her job of collecting medications, removing signs of illness from the death room, stopping to quietly comfort family members.

People spoke to me but their voices seemed to come from far away. My knees felt shaky, my chest ached. I looked at Frank, lying silently in his big bed. He seemed peaceful. *Resting quietly, without pain,* I fantasized. I touched him; his arm and his face were still warm with life. But he was not alive. The shock overtook me and suddenly a deep fog engulfed me—one that would last for several weeks.

In this emotional shock, my senses and responses were dazed. However, this fog allowed me to survive the first hours, even the first few days. I knew I was mourning, grieving my loss, but it all seemed unreal.

After the death you cry, you talk with those around you, you make decisions, notify people, try to eat, walk through the house, thank people, and pretend you are somewhat normal. But much, if not all, of what you do comes enveloped in the emotional fog of grief.

How grateful I was that Frank and I had made so many decisions in advance! It took less than five telephone calls to handle the necessary next steps after Frank's death. Once notified, the mortuary already had full instructions. We had worked out a telephone tree in advance so notification to other friends and family would happen quickly and as gently and personally as possible. One phone call triggered that notification list. Frank was a public figure and we had prepared his obituary weeks before, and someone on our list notified the press and media. One call.

All went smoothly without the extra stress that denial would have caused at this difficult time. Even in my fog I recognized what our earlier preparation had provided to make these first hours more bearable. Many times I quietly thanked Frank for his courage in making those many decisions in advance. He was dead but his love and protection continued to embrace me.

I knew this journey was far from complete. There was a long, uphill road ahead, and I would stumble along this path in the fog. Eventually, I hoped to walk out of this period of grief with new understanding, strength, and memories to hold gently for the rest of my life. I didn't know how long it would take but I understood Frank would be my role model for courage and dignity in the tough times ahead.

In that early morning of death, before Frank was taken from his bed, his room, our home and my life, I stared into his face for the last time. As I touched him and said goodbye, I searched his face for the inner strength I needed to go on without him. "I will miss you so much, Hon. You have been the best part of my life. I hope you're not afraid. Please be safe." I touched his beard, the thin fingers of his hands.

I had told Frank before that I would be fine. I had said it then and believed it. Now the reality of his death had undermined that belief. But in spite of my doubts, I reassured him again. "See how well I'm doing? You've helped make me strong. You'll always be with me. Always."

Maybe these last tender moments; these final lingering touches would help restore my lost bravery. *Stroke, stroke. Maybe, maybe.*

EIGHT

Saying Goodbye

W hen I think of saying permanent goodbyes to a loved one, I tend to separate these farewells into three different categories. First, if one is lucky, there are the goodbyes *before* death that allow you to speak to each other and share the parting. Second, are the goodbyes at the actual time of death. And last, there are the ongoing expressions of goodbye that are manifested in ceremonies such as memorial services, funerals, wakes, the scattering of ashes, the placement of a headstone, and other public and private rituals. Many of these observances go on long after the death of a loved one.

Not everyone is fortunate to say goodbye in all three of these ways. Death may come unexpectedly with no time to say mutual goodbyes. Or the actual moment of death may come when loved ones are far away or sleeping or rushing to the bedside from another city or state. But whatever the timing or setting, saying goodbye is a profound and necessary step in the grieving process and it will likely need to happen more than once.

The gift of a terminal diagnosis is the opportunity to fully say goodbye if the patient and the family do not escape into denial. Accepting the painful truth of impending death will allow time to say goodbye in person, in writing, by phone, on video camera. Accepting the truth means being free to express thoughts and fears and feelings that would otherwise be left unspoken forever. There is so much that can be shared.

In the early weeks and months of my grief, I clung to those final conversations with Frank before he died, savoring every word, expression, and touch. How grateful I was to have his words of love and parting to support me. We said goodbye in a hundred ways and I found a thousand avenues of comfort flowing from those priceless memories. And I believe strongly that our goodbyes brought comfort to Frank as well.

I had made Frank a promise, a sworn pledge months before he died. Once he had died and he was taken from the house, no one would see him again. Frank wanted to be "remembered as a person not a corpse." He felt strongly about it and I respected his last wish. For Frank it was a matter of personal dignity. How could I do less than he asked? No viewing, no visitors, no one. Not even me. I had promised him.

The day Frank died, nine family members and close friends stood around his bed and we all cried together. We were the witnesses to his death. Soon after, two close friends arrived to be part of this little band of mourners. Now it was time for each of us to have our personal and private goodbyes. There would not be a later opportunity.

We all left the bedroom and gathered downstairs. Then by ones and twos Frank's loved ones went back to his upstairs bedroom to have their personal partings. The time was theirs to do and say what they wished, there was no rush. I have never discussed our farewells with the others who were part of that early morning. It all felt too private to share. However, now I am sharing it for the first time, more than seven years later, because I feel it is so important to allow yourself time to say goodbye.

On that October morning I was the last one to say my goodbyes to Frank. More than an hour had passed since his moment of death. I knew the final warmth of life would be just about gone from his body. When I touched him there was no room for pretense or denial. Yet, I found myself on my knees on the bed beside him, as I had been for several hours before he died. I told Frank *everything* I was feeling. I talked of love and gratitude and loneliness and the fog that surrounded me. Gently I locked my fingers in his for the last time. I put a wisp of his hair carefully back in place and stroked his wonderful, gray Hemingway-like beard. I touched his closed eyes. Out loud, I spoke those private words that we had shared in special moments for twenty years. I could almost feel him smile! After about fifteen minutes I slowly unlocked our fingers, said goodbye, and kissed him—for the very last time. As I left his bed, I imprinted in my memory his silent, pain-free, adored face. Then, one step at a time, I inched away from him, never taking my eyes from his face as I left.

Once in the hallway, I closed the door. My breathing felt irregular, tears blurred my vision, my feet felt leaden. I stood in the hall, unsure of my ability to walk or navigate down the stairs. Lost in my emotional fog, I sat down on the hall bench, trying to remember what was expected of me next. *How can I find the strength to join the others downstairs?* I sat motionless, waiting for mobility and some sense of direction to return. Finally, I stood, faced the stairs and began the lonely, weary journey to the bottom of the steps.

I had barely reached the comforting arms of my family

when the hearse from the mortuary arrived. I stepped outside, greeted the two men, thanked them, and told them we would be ready in five minutes. Back inside the house, I gathered our loved ones in the den, closed the two doors to the room and we waited. Out of sight of their arrival and departure, the mortuary men took Frank's body from the house. Weeks earlier, a mortuary counselor had strongly advised me not to watch the removal of Frank's body. Following their experienced advice I had decided I did not want a gurney and a body bag to be my last memories of my beloved husband. I am certain that was sound advice, for me. But I will never forget the sounds as the men struggled down the long flight of stairs, rolled past the den door, down the entry hall, and then closed the front door behind them. Those sounds have always translated into my imagined pictures of Frank leaving the house. That morning those sounds through the door caused me to cry out in anguish. Frank's best friend came to my side, held me, and calmed my shaking. Within me I silently lamented, *Goodbye, goodbye, my love.*

"If you miss the train I'm on you will know that I am gone. You can hear the whistle blow a hundred miles."

The quartet sang the 1960s Peter, Paul, and Mary folk song. Several hundred people gathered to honor Frank and publicly say goodbye. Months earlier Frank and I had planned the services together. He had chosen the speakers and the music. I had suggested using the wonderful video film from his retirement dinner. With slight edits it would be perfect. Frank agreed. The printed memorial program held our shared ideas.

Frank would have been pleased with the stories and expressions of affection and respect. He would have been overwhelmed by the number of people who came to say goodbye. Individuals from all walks of life who knew and cared about Frank gathered together. Welfare mothers, judges, people from the disability community, political leaders, doctors, waitresses, university professors, carpenters— they all came. This memorial service was the celebration of Frank's life as well as a way for the many people in his life to demonstrate their respect and to formally bid Frank farewell. I was pleased that I was able to give them a place to do so.

Surprisingly I felt serene as the service progressed. Maybe it was because I was watching all of Frank's planning unfold or maybe it was because I had been saying goodbye for a year *before* Frank's death. Perhaps I needed to be calm in such a public place and as a public figure. I had cried myself out in the previous four days, yet tears came once again as the quartet sang the words, "Lord, I can't go home this-a-way." My younger son, Mark, held my hand. I looked at the ring he wore, the ring Frank had given him. I had given this same ring to Frank but when Frank's hands became so thin that he could no longer wear it, he wanted Mark to have it. My son recognized what had happened in that moment as I quickly looked away from his hand, and he gently patted my arm.

Saying goodbye happens in so many ways.

And that, for me, is the message of memorial services, wakes, funerals, celebrations of life, and all the ceremonial ways we say goodbye after a death. These parting rituals are as personal and as unique as the people they memorialize. From ashes cast on ocean waves, to a small family ceremony in a forest clearing, to a traditional funeral with a satin-lined casket, to a life celebration with jazz and jokes, to a flag-draped coffin and the playing of taps—there is only one right way to say goodbye, *your* way.

Planning such a ceremony can be healing. Choosing the music, photographs, poetry, speakers, an urn, a special location, flowers, even preparing the printed program. These decisions for and about your loved one can bring comfort and the beginning of closure at a time when you feel alone and unanchored. This is one more way to help you face the parting.

But in the end, no matter how you memorialize the one who has died, saying goodbye is difficult. Regardless of how many times or how many ways you say goodbye, it is physically and emotionally wrenching.

However, that does not mean you should avoid this important step. For even after all the initial goodbyes and the larger public ceremonies, you can find value and comfort in your own private farewell rituals. It may be those times when you take flowers to the cemetery. You may need some personal ceremony when you part with his clothing or when you sell her car or give away his golf clubs. Each night before you go to sleep you may need to read from her favorite book or put his wallet under your pillow. You may turn on a night light in a child's bedroom even though the child is gone. These personal acts will help you say goodbye and may feel like an emotional beacon in your personal darkness.

You need private time to grieve alone. Weeping is essential in these first stages of mourning. Many survivors facing a difficult loss find that photographs help with the grieving process. I created a small photo album with about fifty pictures of Frank. I would sit in his big chair, leafing through the album, smiling and weeping at the same time. For more than two years I kept the album of photographs on my bedside table. Gradually my need for visual reassurance of his place in my life grew less and I moved the album to a dresser drawer near my bed. It remains there today.

Other photographs and mementos helped me feel closer to Frank as I adjusted to his death. I kept Frank's wallet and glasses close. I had his razor in my bathroom for a long time. I even had the dosage spoon we used for Frank's pain medication in a small covered dish in the kitchen for months and months. The same pattern was true with my father after his death. My father's slippers are still in the back of my closet. I framed the eulogy I wrote for my father and placed a special rose from his memorial service under the glass with his photograph. Whatever it takes to feel close will ease your sense of being alone and adrift.

Keepsakes and photographs and pieces of clothing and letters and cards from your loved one can all help with the grieving process. These personal and private sources of comfort are critical to your emotional well-being and to your healing. Please don't try to "tough it out" or bury your grief. Feelings do not disappear just because you ignore them. Grief waits its turn and will not go away until it has been heard. Saying goodbye also means listening to the inner voice of your grief.

Seldom does someone die leaving only a single survivor. And because we usually share the loss of a loved one with other family members and friends, the grieving process can also be a shared experience.

The first Christmas after Frank's death, the members of our immediate family each brought a special ornament for my Christmas tree and the ornaments have thereafter been referred to as "Frank's ornaments." Seashells, sailboats, a small bird house, a heart, a blue bird, a dolphin. One by one we ceremoniously hung them on the tree that first Christmas Eve with some amount of tears. That first year it had only been two months since Frank's death and our shared grief was very fresh. We knew we needed to acknowledge both his absence and his presence on this first Christmas without him.

There have been many shared grieving experiences on birthdays, holidays, and the anniversary of Frank's death each year. Some of us have gone together to take flowers. Two of us traveled together and rode on the ferries of the San Juan Islands in Washington State where Frank sailed for so many years. We visit a tree planted in his honor on Oregon's state capital grounds. A number of us work together on a scholarship foundation in Frank's honor at Portland State University where he taught for more than thirty years. We have grieved together and celebrated together. All of this has helped in the healing process, helped in saying goodbye.

When a loved one dies, those of us who are left behind

are often thought of as survivors. Yet, to really survive, to come out healed and whole after a difficult grieving process requires work. I do not know if you can ever fully mend when someone you love has died but I now know that you can be happy again, laugh once more, enjoy music, spring flowers, and discover reasons to start anew. You can begin to recall memories of the one you loved without feeling great pain. You can eventually put away some of the photographs and mementos. Special dates will begin to pass with only quiet recognition. Music you shared together can once again be enjoyed without tears—most of the time. And one day you will recognize that the tears and pain, the sense of being unanchored, your once gray world, have gone away. You have come through the fog and the relentless seas of grief. You are truly a survivor in a world alive with sunshine, color, and tomorrows.

Until that healing time comes, remember there is no time limit on your personal farewells. A private ceremony on the death anniversary, or on a birthday or a wedding anniversary, is all part of saying goodbye. Do these personal acknowledgments for as long as you need to. You may need to keep "waving" until your loved one is finally out of sight.

NINE

Permission to be Weird

I have a hundred secrets about grieving. Some people may think my secrets are strange. I do not tell my secrets about grieving to anyone because they might think my secrets are too weird. How do I know they are weird? Because I have heard these judgments about grief and how it is supposed to work hundreds of times throughout my life. And so, I have a hundred secrets. My secrets are about trying to cope with the huge hole in my life where my husband and others I have loved and lost used to be.

My secrets are about trying to hold on when I feel I am

sinking. These secrets are my crutches that help me limp through painful days and weeks. My secrets are small pin-points of color in a gray world of grief. And they are about being weird. I know because *they* say so. "They" are the people who judge what is "appropriate" and "inappropriate" when grieving. I have heard them say:

> *"Did you know she keeps his urn on the mantle? Isn't that weird?"*

> *"His wife has been gone for two years and he still takes flowers to her grave every weekend. That's really weird."*

> *"I used her master bathroom at the birthday party and she still has John's slippers sitting in there. That's weird."*

> *"Well, I'll tell you what's weird. She sits in his big chair in the dark and plays his old records."*

I met a man on a train between Portland, Oregon and Boston, Massachusetts. He had the sleeper compartment across from mine. He was probably in his early seventies, and was traveling to visit his children. When he introduced himself, I immediately knew. I could see it in his eyes. *Grief.* But I didn't ask. He was a stranger.

When dinnertime came he knocked and asked if I would like to share dinner with him. In the dining car it took less than five minutes to learn he had been widowed only four months. "I feel lost and unanchored," he admitted over dinner. I told him my husband had died a year and a half earlier. And then I just listened. He knew, somehow, that I was a safe person to talk to. Before long I knew his wife's name, her favorite color, and the name of the disease that killed her. He told me about their home and their children and her funeral. He even talked about the widows who were already pursuing him and how he wasn't ready yet.

The next day we shared lunch and then he told me. He had some secrets. Back at his home near Spokane, Washington in the bedroom they had shared for decades, he had placed a picture of his wife on the dresser. He had surrounded the picture with some of her costume jewelry and sprayed her cologne on the dresser scarf. "I don't want you to think I'm crazy," he explained. "I'm not, am I?"

Then he went on to tell me that on their wedding anniversary—it would have been their forty-eighth—he bought her a beautiful bouquet of roses. He put them beside the picture on the scarf that smelled like her. He wished her a happy anniversary, told her he loved her, then wept for a long, long time. "Do you think I'm crazy? Is this so weird," he asked, "that I should be concerned?"

"Of course not, you're fine, you're just grieving," I reassured him. "We have to do something to cope with our loss on these special days. It's not weird, it's wonderful!"

Four months dead after more than four decades together. A man takes flowers to his wife to commemorate a wedding anniversary and then worries about his sanity and the appropriateness of his expression of love! What is it about our culture that would make him believe he is acting crazy?

In the past few years since Frank's death I have become part of a secret society, a club of widows and widowers who feel safe to share their stories of loss and mourning and grief *and* their special secrets. Sometimes that club includes parents who have lost a child, a son grieving for his father, a gay man coping with the death of a twenty-five year partner. I have heard many secrets from those facing the loss of a loved one. Repeatedly, people will preface their secrets with, "I know this will sound weird...."

Never before have I been privileged to the secrets of so many wonderful and caring people. I am convinced, more than ever, that our culture has labeled as "weird" some of the most wonderful, precious, and sensitive acts of grieving and love imaginable. Now I understand, it is imperative to give ourselves permission to grieve in our own time and in our own way. Our culture's labels of what is weird and what is appropriate when grieving are hurtful and harmful. We may choose to keep our secrets but we need not feel strange about choosing our own path for grieving. Or we may decide to tell part of our secrets so that others may learn from them and may know they are not alone.

In the early weeks following Frank's death, I attended a holiday gathering that had been a tradition for us for several years. It was a meal followed by Christmas caroling through the host and hostess's neighborhood. I had almost skipped the evening but I decided it might help me to be outside enjoying the event, an event Frank had always found so special. So I went. Good food, good company, lots of hugs and sympathy, *and* a holiday gift I could never have imagined. When the caroling was over and we came back to the house to warm up, a woman I barely knew asked if she could speak to me privately. I agreed. She first told me she had seen my husband's obituary and knew he had been cremated. And she also knew from a family member that Frank was not to be interred until after Christmas.

She had become a young widow eight years earlier. Now she wanted to share with me a suggestion offered to her by an older widow the day following the death of the younger woman's husband. "You'll think this is weird but it may really help you in the time ahead," my new acquaintance explained gently. She suggested that before I placed Frank's urn permanently, I remove some of his ashes and put them in a small lidded container that I could keep with me at home. She said, "You'll be glad later that you did this."

Two days later I returned Frank's urn to the mausoleum accompanied by a small silver box. I told them what I wanted and they didn't even flinch. That night I sat on my bed alone with a large white napkin spread out before me. In the middle of the napkin was the small silver box. I shook it gently and something rattled. Almost like metal on metal, only more subtle. I hesitated. Then I removed the tight lid from the box and looked inside.

From that moment on there was no doubt that these were Frank's remains. On top of the small mound of ashes was a piece of burned wire attached to what appeared to be a small piece of bone. I paused, then I smiled. Frank had been ill a long time and suffered from years of pain. He had two separate pain control mechanisms imbedded in his body. They were expensive electronic devices with wires, some attached to vertebrae in his back. For years, Frank had laughed about selling his body for parts when he died. We kidded him about being the Bionic Man.

And here it was—a small piece of burned wire. I picked it up, examined the wire and then placed it back in the silver box. My Bionic Man. This was Frank—or part of him. I touched the ashes gently, and then closed the special little box.

That silver box with the silver seashell on top has traveled with me across the country. In the early months of grieving I carried the silver box in my briefcase when I traveled, feeling him close at hand. When I moved east the silver box traveled with me by train, across America. It has been on my bedroom dresser for years. In more than seven years it has been opened only four times...on two wedding anniversaries and on two other occasions.

I never had an opportunity to thank the woman from the party, but my holiday gift from her in 1993 has been a priceless one. Maybe one day I will not need the silver box anymore. Maybe one day I will spread those ashes on the waters of the San Juan Islands where we sailed together for twenty years. But I am not ready yet. The silver box and its contents still give me comfort. Sometimes I pick the box up and shake it gently as I walk in or out of the bedroom. I listen to the small sound of metal on metal. And I smile and sigh and Frank feels closer.

There are millions of secrets—secrets about grief
hidden by those afraid of being judged weird
or strange or even worse.

In the mausoleum where my husband's ashes rest (a place that felt cold and foreign when my grandparents and father were placed there), years of regular visits have helped me understand the commonality of grief. Sometimes a new name appears on the marble and after the first flowers wilt there is no sign of visitors again. While other crypts tell the story of every family event and flowers appear weekly.

Parents, spouses, sons and daughters, grandchildren, and special friends "speak" to those who have died. Sometimes they speak out loud. I have heard them. Sometimes they speak with flowers. But it is the other "messages" that catch my breath or bring me to tears. Balloons and birthday cards, a lace-trimmed handkerchief, the picture of a new grandchild born only weeks after a forty-six year old woman was placed near Frank. A stuffed, soft lamb at Easter for a one-year old child and a Batman toy for a seven-year old on a two-foot high Christmas tree. Poems, anniversary cards, news clippings, wedding photos, lipstick marks on marble, apology notes, Valentine's cards, graduation announcements, and love letters speak to the dead.

Everyone grieves in their own time
and in their own way.

I have learned so much about grieving from those "messages." People need to reach out and speak to those who have died. I know their need to share with those they love. Death does not end love—or need. If our culture thinks this behavior is weird, that it represents instability or wishful thinking or desperation, I would challenge this judgment. This grieving behavior represents love and loss and coping and healing. This mourning is necessary and normal, it is real and it is not rare.

People who are grieving have hundreds of secrets. Many of us would like to tell our secrets to others if they could be gentle, understanding, and tolerant. We want others to understand how we grieve, how we cope, and not judge us. Their acceptance would help us and ease our pain a little. But, when all is said and done, people who are grieving do not need approval from others. We have given ourselves permission to be weird, to comfort ourselves. We will heal one secret at a time.

TEN

Grieving Into Healing

Please make the hurting stop! Make the
loneliness go away. I can't face any more pain.
I can't go on without the one I love!

Grief is hard to bear. It feels as if you will never be whole again. The permanence of death and the finality of the loss can leave you feeling as if you can never be happy again. And to some degree that is true. You will never be able to share happy times again with the deceased person you love so. The memories, pictures, and perhaps some belongings are all you have left. And for a long time, these memories and mementos may bring you more pain than comfort.

But while grief is a difficult experience, there is much to be learned from those who have been through the work of grieving, facing the pain and finally learning to live again. This journey will be unique for each of us, yet there are common patterns that define the experience. Ida Fischer's pamphlet, "Widow's Guide to Life," labels the four stages of grief that are so often the pattern.

- ◆ Shock and numbness
- ◆ Searching and yearning
- ◆ Disorientation and disorganization
- ◆ Reorganization

While there is frequently an overlapping of these stages and some slippage back and forth into each stage, this pattern is as near to a blueprint for the grieving process as I have found.

– SHOCK AND NUMBNESS –

During this phase your emotions will be constantly on the surface and nearly impossible to control. You may not be able to fully concentrate and later, looking back, you will find you are unable to recall much that occurred in those first days and weeks. Sleep may come with great difficulty or, the reverse; you may want to sleep all the time. Your appetite can disappear. Reading will be a chore and retention almost impossible.

Physical symptoms in this first phase of grieving may include dry mouth and skin, a hollow feeling in your stomach, exhaustion, a frequent need for deep sighs in order to get enough oxygen to your lungs. Loud noises will startle you as if you are being awakened from a fitful sleep. You will feel you are in a fog. You might even experience a sense of being mentally unstable. This is often a period of confusion, depression, and anxiety. All of these reactions are defenses for your mind and body to help protect you against the extreme pain that the reality of death brings. You won't *feel* normal but, in fact, this stage is both normal and necessary when grieving.

– SEARCHING AND YEARNING –

This phase usually lasts for months, maybe longer. You will see your loved one's face in a crowded store, going around a corner, driving by in a car. You look for them and it feels impossible to face the reality that you will not see him or her again. You yearn for his voice, her touch. Then you begin to believe you have forgotten what your loved one looks like. Oh, how you need them to help you through this terrible adjustment! Feelings of abandonment and anger may dominate for awhile. Express your anger. Say out loud what you are holding inside. And do not stop crying, it may help relieve some of your anger.

This yearning and searching stage of grief is a trying and wearing period and, in all honesty, a phase that some of your friends and family will not understand. You will have to work hard to finally admit to yourself and accept that you will not find the one you search for.

– DISORIENTATION AND DISORGANIZATION –

This phase of grieving tends to be a period of strong depression. It seems to come as one moves from the early confused, lost, foggy period where death is not yet a reality to the beginning of acceptance and moving on. For me, it came after six months of being almost solely focused on the past and my life with my late husband. As the early healing began to happen I took my first look toward my future life alone. It was like hitting a brick wall emotionally. It felt as if I turned my back on all we had together. I dropped into a deep pit of depression. No energy, food seemed tasteless, and simple decisions like what clothing to wear each morning often seemed stressful and complicated. I felt distant from those around me. I had believed I was doing better and now, again, I experienced feelings as if I was back at square one. I could not continue looking backward and yet I could not bear to look forward.

This emotional brick wall blocked me at six months and once again at the first anniversary of Frank's death. Both times I did not expect it. It was very disturbing to feel myself slipping back into a world of gray. Facing these cycles of grief was some of the hardest work of my life. At last I understood that my grief was not something to deny or hide or bury. Nor could I rush the healing. Somehow I knew I could not ignore the pain if I ever expected to heal. The slippage into depression came less often after a year, and even less after two years, but it took a long time before I began to emerge from my grieving and feel somewhat whole again. Glimmers of hope hinted that I might once again be happy.

– REORGANIZATION –

The fourth stage of grieving Fischer describes is one I think of as "recovery." My first glimpses of recovery were more than two years after Frank's death. One day while watching some college students have a snowball fight, I found myself laughing again, actually laughing out loud. Occasionally I would hum as I worked around the house or drove in the car. Snippets of fun and excitement and anticipation returned—not often—but they began to resurface. My former high energy levels returned. Making plans for my future filled more of my thoughts. I wanted to write, to listen to music again, and to talk about Frank without crying. Even a stop at my local flower shop no longer reminded me of the smell of a funeral.

Still, I faced difficult days that seemed to come without apparent reason. Special days like birthdays and wedding anniversaries remained sad and heavy. Sometimes I was overwhelmed with loneliness for Frank. News of a friend would still make me reach for the telephone wanting to share the news with Frank.

When the time came, I decided to sell our home in Oregon, the house we chose together in our first months of marriage. It was surprisingly traumatic. Although we had not lived in the house for several years before his death each room held memories, each closet and home improvement project was about our life together. My younger son, Mark, who now lived in the house, painted and wallpapered with me as we prepared the house for sale. Mark held me and comforted me when tears came during the several weeks' process. One more part of letting go.

Sunsets, such a strong reminder of our many years of sailing together, made me especially lonely. The outdoor smells of morning always brought thoughts of Frank. Driving in the rain, listening to the sound of wipers on the windshield, made him seem close by. These experiences had brought tears for all those early months of grieving. Now as I began to heal I found these same experiences reminded me of him yet prompted a smile instead.

Recovery had been painful and slow but it was surely

more of a reality with each passing week. I took flowers to Frank less frequently. The photo album I'd made of his pictures would sometimes need dusting from lack of handling. Personal items of his I had kept for almost four years were finally discarded. His battered blue bag, long carried on his wheelchair, prompted tears as I put it in a large plastic garbage sack—but I was ready to let it go. The week I moved into my new home, his leg braces received one final hug before I parted with them forever. He would have thought I was silly to have kept them so long, but I could picture his feet, his face, and his courage each time I looked at those braces. They were a powerful memory for me. But now I found the memory of his brave struggle quite strong and intact without this symbol of his painful disability.

Steadily I was progressing in my healing—beginning with hesitant baby steps, now striding toward my future. What had seemed impossible in the beginning felt feasible as the four-year anniversary approached. I had learned so much, experienced so many changes, overcome so many hurdles. It had been the hardest challenge of my life but I felt as if the puzzle pieces that had once been *me* were finally fitting back together. Now I longed to see the sunshine again. I craved to see the view of the rest of my life from the vantage point of the "healed."

ELEVEN

The Long, Slow Climb Back

Sometimes I feel as if I am returning to Earth after a seven-year voyage into space. I am uncertain of where I have been but I know it has been a remarkable journey. The capsule of grief that hurled me headlong into the unknown has been womb-like, isolating me from my familiar world until the time came to return.

My journey has certainly not been without risk, pain, and adjustment. It has been an experience almost impossible to describe to those who have not faced the ordeal of death and heavy grief. A *Newsweek* reader, Ann Brener, shared her description artfully in a letter to the editor: "When we grieve passionately, we forge a new contract with life. No one signs up to walk the mourner's path. Many find unexpected depth and richness in its healing journey."

This road to healing is a long, slow climb back.
You cannot rush it. You must not ignore it.

Until you have worked through your loss, faced your grief, and seriously worked at healing, you will have either an open wound or a festering internal injury waiting to resurface. The grieving begins one step at a time, one day at a time. Do not expect too much of yourself, at least for awhile. Do not be afraid to be gentle with yourself. You deserve time to limp until you are strong enough to walk again. No one else can dictate your path or your timetable. Grieving is a private, individual passage. If you are fortunate, those who care about you will give support, in large part by respecting your pace for healing. But, the truth is, you mostly go it alone.

During the years I worked on this book I struggled through the sadness of my personal memories. However, writing this book turned out to be a critical tool in my healing process. For each of you healing will be a variety of hurdles and mixed levels of personal support. The healing will never happen quickly enough. Your pain will never stop soon enough. Your loss will always remain with you, as will your special memories. Your life will be changed forever by death. But, in spite of your loss, there will be a new depth and richness about you. And it will come one day at a time, one step at a time.

There will be no sign on the road indicating you have reached the place of the "healed." In fact, you may be *there* for awhile before you recognize your arrival. For too long you have felt vulnerable, alone, sad, and somewhat adrift. Your nearly healed self may not expect to feel differently. You can easily miss the mileposts that indicate you are arriving at this happier, healed spot.

I was packing to move back to Oregon. Three years earlier I had accepted a great job at the Kennedy School of Government at Harvard University in Boston. I was now ready to go home to Oregon. I would first sell "our" home and buy a new house of my own. I knew I was returning to a place that was all about my late husband. I would have to face the places he had worked, the homes we had shared, the special place where we were married, the location where he died.

Packing cups and saucers one night I suddenly realized that thoughts of these places no longer brought pain and tears. Instead, I smiled as thoughts of these familiar places awakened images of Frank. No tears came, only feelings of warmth. I continued packing—towels, pans, and photo albums. We were going home! For me, to continue my life with a major transition behind me. For Frank, special memories of him that I would carry with me for the rest of my life.

Three years earlier I had arrived on the East Coast sad and lonely. I had clung to my photo album of Frank. His bathrobe hung on my bedroom door. My little silver box with his ashes was next to my bed. I never listened to music and I dreaded holidays. In my mind, I was clearly his "wife" and not his "widow." In those first years I cried easily and laughed infrequently. Now, three years later, I was a different person. How far I had come!

As I continued packing, music from the sound track of the film *Sleepless in Seattle* played in the background. I giggled at the song "Back in the Saddle Again." Yes, maybe I was even ready for dating again. It was a scary prospect but felt possible now.

Over the next few days, packing and sorting, I set aside a number of items for a local charity—things I no longer needed. Moving can certainly be a way to unclutter your life, lighten your load. But more than the books and shoes, pans, and end tables I was giving away, I was also leaving behind other significant things that had arrived with me three years ago. Much of the sadness was now behind me. I was about to set aside loneliness even when I was alone. There were still times of melancholy, but I was no longer actively grieving. When I had come to Boston in the spring of 1995 my loss was relatively new and grief was an intimate part of my daily life. Now, three years later, healing had become a reality. There was a time when I felt this would never happen for me.

While Tammy Wynette crooned "Stand By Your Man" in the background, I knew I had. I had stood by Frank through our twenty-year marriage, during the years of his illness, throughout the months and weeks and hours of his dying process—I had been there with him and for him. And I had stood by his memory for four years—with love and respect. One day at a time, one step at a time, I had made the long, slow climb back. Now I was ready to take the final steps that would reflect the hard work of the last four years.

I sealed a packed box and perhaps, at the same time, gently packed away in my heart the pain that had been such an immediate part of my life all these years since Frank's terminal diagnosis. I was moving home, moving on. This was what I needed. Frank would have wanted this, and now, at last, I wanted it, too.

TWELVE

Death Takes Center Stage

On the subject of death and grieving,
silence is not golden.

As people face a terminal illness, as they deal with the pain of mourning, as they cope with the long journey of grieving, silence adds to their isolation and confusion and suffering. Those of us who have experienced this personal trauma have an obligation to reach out and to speak up. If our culture is ever going to treat the dying process with respect and openness, we must not be afraid to speak frankly about what we have experienced.

For instance, hospice programs and what they do are unknown or poorly understood by many who need their services. Those of us who have been privileged to have a loved one die under the care and support of hospice must share this experience with our family and friends, in our church, our civic clubs, our communities. We should consider volunteering and the importance of contributing to help make hospice more available and better understood.

For those who have walked the mourner's path, we must not be afraid to visit those who are dying and speak openly with them and their family members about our own experiences. Sharing our own stories will help others understand the grieving process and the need to be patient and kind with themselves and others who are still suffering through *their* period of mourning. We can reach out and give support to neighbors and friends and work associates when we learn they have lost a loved one to death. Remember how isolating it was when no one wanted us to talk about our loss? We cannot let this pattern be repeated. It is not good enough to simply send a sympathy card. Visit. Call. Reach out. Give them a chance to talk with someone who understands.

When you hear discussions that label those in grief as if they are "weird," speak up and tell them your experience about the grieving process. It is a perfect opportunity to educate the unaware. Suggest the topic of grief to a local radio or television talk show. You could educate hundreds, even thousands, of people during one show. Be willing to share your personal experiences.

Watch for newspaper stories that perpetuate the myth that grieving can be or should be over in just a few weeks or months. Take advantage of a letter to the editor column to correct this misconception of the grief process. Tell it like it is! For, in truth, does anyone ever completely "get over" the death of a loved one? I do not think so.

The openings for educating and helping others, by speaking out and telling the story of this traumatic human experience are all around us. Our culture could be changed if each one of us committed ourselves to the message of death with dignity and grief as a visible part of the life experience. For me, this book is part of that commitment.

Recently on a plane trip I sat next to a man who told me how worried his wife was about her mother. The source of her concern was related to the fact that her seventy-five-year-old mother was still depressed and very sad a year after her husband's death! I turned to my seat mate, looked him square in the eye and told him that after four years I was just reaching a place I could describe as "healed." He looked very surprised. I went on to tell him what I had learned from others and from my own personal experiences. I suggested some things that might help his mother-in-law. "Let her tell you about her sadness. Hold her when she cries. She misses being held. Keep a picture of her husband in your home so she feels you still share her love for him. Encourage her to talk about him over coffee in the morning or on an evening walk or in the car. Don't forget their wedding anniversary... she won't."

The man kept nodding as if in disbelief as I continued. "Ask her if you can take her to the cemetery on his birthday or Memorial Day. You can help her work through her grief instead of hiding it," I explained gently. He and I parted at the airport with his words, "This may be the most valuable lesson of my adult life." That may or may not be true but I do believe some older woman in Atlanta now has a more understanding and supportive family. I never miss such an opportunity.

There is little question that the issues surrounding death and grieving are receiving strong new focus in America. As science and the medical arena have found new tools to keep the severely ill alive, debates have surfaced about extreme measures, natural death, "unplugging" patients, and physician-assisted death. Pain control has been a major component of these conversations. These debates and discussions will continue for many years to come.

End-of-life pain control has prompted conflict in the medical community, in the caregiving community, and even in Congress. The fact is, some medications given to keep a dying patient pain-free in the last days and hours of his life, may also hasten death. As a patient approaches death, most feel that it is humane and compassionate to use the necessary pain medications to prevent suffering. Others argue that any medications that hasten death, even by a few hours, are unacceptable.

Recent pain control legislation in Congress that has attempted to place controls on the use of pain medication and to hold physicians criminally liable for certain levels of dosage, has caused national outcries from many in the medical community. Organizations wanting to keep terminally ill patients from unnecessary suffering include The American Cancer Society, and the National Hospice and Palliative Care Organization, among others. There is also great concern that the fear of criminal sanctions causes doctors to withhold needed pain medication from dying patients, leaving them in anguish and pain in their last days and hours.

It is important to speak early with your doctor about his or her attitudes and practices on end-of-life pain control. Many patients are more anxious about pain than about death. Knowing that your medical caregiver will not let you suffer needlessly can be a great comfort to the dying and their loved ones. Do not be afraid to raise this issue with your doctor. You have a right to know.

As a former Oregon governor, I am in a unique position to speak to another area of national medical controversy regarding end-of-life choices and decisions. Oregon is the only state in the nation to have a physician-assisted death law in place having passed on the ballot in 1994, and operational since 1998. However, my observations on this law are more than just the circumstances of my residence in Oregon and my former political office.

My husband, a respected state senator, introduced to the state legislature what would become the Oregon "Death With Dignity" law. Three times he introduced it, three times it failed. Frank believed in the law but understood that his fellow legislators found it a tough political vote. Finally, Oregon voters passed the law as a ballot initiative—not once, but twice—the second time with a 60 percent majority.

In the first three years of its use, only seventy Oregonians used the act—seventy citizens out of the 90,000 who died in Oregon during that three-year period. Even those who may oppose the law can recognize that Oregon citizens have used the law sparingly. The many safeguards and guidelines in the "Death With Dignity" law have allowed its implementation without complications. Oregonians, mostly cancer patients, who have used the law to hasten their death have achieved humane and peaceful deaths at home surrounded by loved ones.

As Frank approached the end of his life, he longed for release from his massive deterioration. Tired and bedridden, he felt little quality remained in his life. How he wished for "his law" to be in place. He died in October 1993 without access to Oregon's "Death With Dignity" law. The ballot measure passed in 1994.

In his final months of life, Frank found comfort in the fact that the ballot initiative was moving forward even though he understood it would not be available in time to help end his suffering. But now, other Oregon residents have that choice.

Physician-assisted death is controversial in this country but in Oregon our experience with the law has caused citizens' attitudes to grow more supportive with each year of the law's use. Perhaps most importantly, Oregon's law has brought the dying process out of the closet for patients, physicians, politicians, and families. Regardless of where someone stands on the issue, there is open, ongoing dialogue. At last, differences can be aired. What we can talk about, we can make better.

Oregon is a national leader in the percentage of terminally ill patients enrolled in hospice programs. Oregon's morphine utilization rate for end-of-life pain control is among the highest nationally. Oregon physicians have demonstrated their support for necessary pain control. We are considered a model state in end-of-life care.

The record of Oregon's "Death With Dignity" law is one of compassion and caring. Although the national debate may continue for years, there is a special place in my heart for the law and Frank's passionate belief that adults have the knowledge and wisdom to choose. His question was always,

"Doesn't how we die matter as much as how we live?"
Clearly, that will be the question America will debate
for a long time to come.

The AIDS crisis also raised the profile of death and grieving discussions in this country. Television documentaries, movies, newspaper and magazine articles told the moving stories of young adults dying surrounded by friends, some with, some without family members present. The stories were often about courage and dignity associated with the dying process. The survivors marched for AIDS funding, created the AIDS quilt, (several blocks long) and testified before congressional committees pleading for increased research monies. The visible grief of these survivors raised the consciousness of an America unused to being exposed to such public mourning.

Dying and grieving will not return to the closet. We each have an obligation to make certain this is the case. We need not all agree on the issues being debated. Our own experiences and philosophies are varied. However, all humans will die and before that, most of us will experience the death of a loved one and the subsequent painful grieving that follows. It is a long and arduous path from death to a sense of being healed. It is that common and natural experience that deserves greater understanding by this society.

Death and grieving, like birth and life, deserve a scene of their own in our remarkable human drama. We will each play this role at some time. Let the script show we exited without denial and played the final scene with dignity to a compassionate and gentle audience.

Epilogue

On that eventful day in February 2001 when my publisher and I decided we were a good match for the publication of this book, my first "good news" call went to my younger sister, Pat. I could not wait to share my news with her.

Pat understood the pain I had relived to put this book on paper. She knew my hopes that the book's publication would bring comfort and support to others facing death and loss. Now it would be published. I could not wait to tell her.

Pat shared my excitement. We laughed and she teased me about making the Oprah Book Club list next year. The subject of the book was serious. The telephone call, however, was full of laughter. This was the pattern of our life—sharing the good news and the bad times alike. She asked me for the first autographed copy of the book. I promised it would be hers. Many years ago I had learned to share with my baby sister.

Twelve days after that phone call Pat was dead. At sixty-two, she simply dropped dead. Eight years earlier, against terrible odds, Pat had battled and survived a highly aggressive form of lung cancer. When we could finally breathe easier about her health, she was dead.

Instead of beginning the editing process for my book on death and grieving, I first had to write my sister's eulogy. It was not supposed to work this way. My sister and I were supposed to grow old together. Our birthdays were just one day apart, the week before Christmas, and we were supposed to celebrate them together for at least another twenty years. Now, even as I write this epilogue, only six months after her death, I ask myself, *What am I expected to do without her in December? It's not supposed to work this way.*

As I had done for both our parents and both our maternal grandparents, I wrote Pat's eulogy. But for the first time, I didn't ask someone else to read my words at the memorial service. I needed to tell my sister goodbye myself. She had left me without telling me she was going. One of us had to say goodbye. I had always imagined it would be her sending me off. After all, she was my baby sister.

In May, the day before Mother's Day, we buried my sister's urn in the plot with her infant daughter, the daughter who died thirty-nine years earlier in a car accident. Pat's four grown sons and her husband had made the decision about her placement and it felt exactly right. The new headstone with both mother's and daughter's names seemed to complete a circle broken long ago in a tragic accident. This day, they were together again. I knew how much this decision would have pleased Pat.

Standing in the May sunshine beside the grave of my only sister and my only niece I felt a strong sense of my need to let go. *In order for mother and daughter to be together, Pat and I must be apart.* My turn was finished. Silently I called on my own words from Pat's memorial service in March to help me with this wrenching separation—just a few silent sentences from the eulogy I had written and delivered for my sister.

Perhaps no word better describes Pat. She was a gift, a remarkable gift. I remember so many times this gift came wrapped in fancy foil and tied with silken ribbons. And there were the other times—wrapped in plain brown paper, without ribbon or bows but containing the gift of her quiet strength and spirit.

Throughout her lifetime she gave and gave. She asked for little. She demanded nothing. She forgave everything.

As we face our loss, deal with our grief, Pat's absence will create a void that seems permanent. But soon, once we've healed, even a little, she will do what she has always done—fill the voids in our life with love and special memories. That has always been her gift to us.

One of Pat's final gifts to me was the painful and vivid reminder of how each death is unique and each mourner's path is unique. There is no exact formula for grieving and healing. Each person we love occupies a special place in our life and in our heart. We will grieve them like snowflakes— no two alike.

This conclusion to my book comes in the middle of the wintertime of my grief for my younger sister. Eventually, I will emerge into my personal spring feeling partially healed and ready to again experience life's joys. The month or even the year when my spring returns is not yet clear but I know, as I know the daffodil's beauty, that it will come. In its own time and in its own way. And in that spring I will take my sister her autographed book.

Resources

Organizations

American Association of Suicidology
4201 Connecticut Ave., Suite 408
Washington, DC 20008
(202) 237-2280

American Cancer Society
1599 Clifton Rd. N.E.
Atlanta, GA 30329-4251
(404) 320-3333

American Geriatrics Society
350 Fifth Avenue, Suite 801
New York, NY 10118
(212) 308-1414

Association for Death Education
& Counseling (ADEC)
342 N. Main Street
West Hartford, CT 06117
(860) 586-7503

Choice in Dying/Partnership
for Caring
1620 Eye St. N.W., Suite 202
Washington, DC 20006
(202) 296-8071

Compassion in Dying of Oregon
6312 SW Capitol Hwy., Suite 410
Portland, OR 97201
(503) 525-1956

The Compassionate Friends
(death of a child)
900 Jorie Blvd., Suite 78
Oak Brook, IL 60523
(630) 990-0010

Mothers Against Drunk Driving
(MADD)
P.O. Box 541688
Dallas, TX 75354
(800) 483-MADD (victim line)

The National Center for Grieving
Children & Families
A Service of the Dougy Center
for Grieving Children
3909 S.E. 52nd Avenue
Portland, OR 97286
(503) 775-5683

National Hospice and Palliative
Care Organization
1700 Diagonal Rd., Suite 300
Alexandria, VA 22314
(703) 243-5900

Oncology Nursing Society
501 Holiday Dr.
Pittsburgh, PA 15220-2749
(412) 921-7373

Oregon Hospice Association
812 S.W. 10th, Suite 204
Portland, OR 97205
(503) 228-2104

Widowed Person Services
AARP
601 E Street, N.W.
Washington, DC 20049
(202) 434-2277

BOOKS

Don't Let Death Ruin Your Life
—Jill Brooke, Dutton Books, New York, NY (2001)

Final Victory
—Thomas A. Preston, M.D., Prima Publishing, Roseville, CA (2000)

Nobody's Child Anymore
—Barbara Bartocci, Sorin Books, Notre Dame, IN (2000)

Remembrances and Celebrations
—J.W. Harris, Random House, New York, NY (2000)

Handbook for Mortals: Guidance for People Facing Serious Illness
—Joanne Lynn, M.D. and Joan Harrold, M.D., Oxford University Press (1999)

Midlife Orphan
—Jane Brooks, The Berkley Publishing Group, New York, NY (1999)

A Time to Die—The Place for Physician Assistance
—Charles F. McKhann, M.D., Yale University Press, New Haven, CT (1999)

Tear Soup
—Pat Schweibert and Chuck DeKlyen, Grief Watch, Portland, OR (1999)

The Oregon Death With Dignity Act: A Guidebook for Health Care Providers
—The Center for Ethics in Health Care, Oregon Health Sciences University, Portland, OR (1998)

Dying Well: The Prospect for Growth at the End of Life
—Ira Byock, M.D., Putnam/Riverhead, New York, NY (1998)

A Passage Through Grief
—B. Baumgardner, Broadman and Holdman (1997)

The Good Death: The American Search to Reshape the End of Life
—Marilyn Webb, Bantam Books, New York, NY (1997)

On Death and Dying
—Elizabeth Kubler-Ross, M.D., Touchstone, New York, NY (1997)

Tuesdays With Morrie
—Mitch Albom, Doubleday Dell Publishing Group, New York, NY (1997)

Light on Aging and Dying
—Helen Nearing, Harcourt Brace and Company, Orlando, FL (1995)

The Mourning Handbook
—Helen Fitzgerald, A Fireside Book, Simon and Schuster, New York, NY (1994)

Motherless Daughters
—H. Edelman, Bantam Books, New York, NY (1994)

Days of Grace
—A. Ashe, Alfred A. Knopf, New York, NY (1993)

Active Euthanasia, Religion, and the Public Debate
—Par Ridge Center for the Study of Health, Faith, and Ethics, Chicago, IL (1991)

To Heal Again
—Rusty Berkus, Red Rose Press, CA (1984)

WEBSITES

American Association of Suicidology.
www.suicidology.org

American Cancer Society. Resource for cancer research and patient support.
www.cancer.org

Americans for Better Care of the Dying. Joanne Lynne, M.D. and
Joan Harrold, M.D.
www.abcd-caring.org

Choice in Dying and other end-of-life resources including advance directives
for every state.
www.partnershipforcaring.org

Center for Ethics in Health Care, combines the perspectives of health professionals, patients, and families to improve teaching, research and clinical
consultation about ethical issues in patient care and health policy.
www.ohsu.edu/ethics/

Dougy Center for Grieving Children, especially helpful for grieving children
and teens.
www.dougy.org

Growth House, Inc., the Internet's leading online community for end-of-life
care. Includes many related resources, including a book excerpt by author
Marilyn Webb.
www.growthouse.org

Hospice Foundation of America, especially helpful for grief resources.
www.hospicefoundation.org

Mothers Against Drunk Driving, includes victim support resources.
www.madd.org

National Hospice and Palliative Care Organization, includes very useful links
to a number of other groups.
www.nhpco.org

ABOUT THE AUTHOR

A descendant of Oregon Trail pioneers and a fourth generation Oregonian, former Governor Barbara Roberts has carried forth the tradition of trailblazing and innovation. Roberts began her years of public service as an advocate for disabled children while she fought for the educational rights of her autistic son. While Roberts was Governor

Barbara and Frank Roberts

(1991-1995), Oregon was recognized by *Financial World Magazine* as the seventh best-managed state in the nation. Today, Roberts is recognized as a strong advocate for environmental management, a national leader for human and civil rights, and among the nation's foremost "reinventors" of effective government.

Roberts now teaches at Portland State University as an Associate Director of Leadership Development. Prior to that, Governor Roberts had a five-year association with the John F. Kennedy School of Government at Harvard University. In 2001, The Kennedy School of Government at Harvard University honored Roberts with "The Alumni Public Service Achievement Award."

Former Governor Roberts was married to Oregon State Senator Frank Roberts, who died in 1993. She has two adult sons, Mike and Mark Sanders, two grandchildren, and six step-grandchildren ranging in age from four years to twenty-two years old.

NEWSAGE PRESS
TROUTDALE, OREGON

For more information visit our website or call:
877-695-2211
www.newsagepress.com

Distributed to bookstores by Publishers Group West:
800-788-3123